"In the US and the UK, leaders tend to focus solely on their fiduciary reasonability to shareholders. In Japan and China, the focus is broadened to include their obligations to society, employees, and business partners. Many of the problems we have seen over the last fifteen years would have been prevented or minimized if leaders promoted a culture of values and integrity.

"Dr. Betty breaks the mold of traditional books on the subject by including inspirational stories from great leaders who created a high value and high integrity organizations while achieving great results. #Values is a must read for leaders at any level."

~ Carlos Fuentes,
Vice President, Federal Reserve Bank of New York

"Revealing, inspiring, richly rewarding."

~ ABC -20/20

"Values, authenticity, and character shine brightest during times of challenge, uncertainty, and adversity. Dr. Uribe's writings reinforce that doing the right thing may at times be tough in the short term, but consistently pays dividends in the long term, both personally and professionally."

~ Dennis V. Arriola,
Chairman and CEO, Southern California Gas Company

""Before we can decide if a leader is worth following, we have to know what they believe, what they hold dear, and what guides them. In short, we need some sense of their values. There's a quaint word that we don't hear often enough these days: values. Yet values are a critical—if often overlooked—ingredient to the managerial stew we call leadership.

"In her book, #Values: The Secret to Top Level Performance in Business and Life, Dr. Betty Uribe unpacks the reasons some people become good leaders, and those things that keep others from realizing their full leadership potential. Drawing upon the wisdom of "values-based" leaders in both the military and the corporate world, Uribe shows that good leaders started out as good people. Concentrate on creating more of the latter, and we'll find ourselves with more of the former.

"This book is a valuable addition to the existing library on leadership. Dive into it, and you'll emerge with a better understanding not just of leadership but also of something even more mysterious we encounter every day: human nature."

~ Ruben Navarrette Jr.,

Author, *A Darker Shade of Crimson: Odyssey of a Harvard Chicano* Syndicated Columnist, Washington Post Writers Group

"In the US and the UK, leaders tend to focus solely on their fiduciary reasonability to shareholders. In Japan and China, the focus is broadened to include their obligations to society, employees, and business partners. Many of the problems we have seen over the last fifteen years would have been prevented or minimized if leaders promoted a culture of values and integrity.

"#Values is a must-read for anyone trying to build an organization from 'Good to Great.' Dr. Betty Uribe is the right author for a book on Values-Based Leadership!"

~ Stephen Christensen,
Dean of the School of Business, Concordia University

"During challenging and changing times, leaders show their true colors through their #Values. This profound book provides a truly fresh perspective, inspiring stories, and practical tools for creating the kind of world we dream about—where honesty and integrity are in the minds and hearts of all."

~ **Marcia Wieder**,
CEO, Dream University,
Best-Selling Author, *DREAM*
Founder, The Meaning Institute

"Dr. Uribe has created a book to inspire us all to be better leaders and, as a result, better in business. Whether you are a fledgling entrepreneur, a recent MBA graduate, or a seasoned CEO, there is wisdom to be gained from her insightful book. When leaders align their behaviors with meaningful personal values, entire cultures can shift and drive greater success. This is powerful stuff!"

~ **Nina Vaca**,
Chairman & CEO, Pinnacle Group,
Corporate Director, Kohl's Stores,
Cinemark Theatres & Comerica Bank,
Presidential Ambassador, Global Entrepreneurship,
Chairman Emeritus, United States Hispanic
Chamber of Commerce

A Word from the Vatican
Monsignor Giacomo Pappalardo

Greetings!

As I read through and carefully thought about the principles and practices within Dr. Betty Uribe's book, *#Values: The Secret to Top Level Performance in Business and Life,* I must confess my initial difficulty, due in part to a language barrier, and in part to grasping the wholeness of the subjects dealt within the book, which are somewhat different than my specific humanistic-religious studies and area of expertise.

However, after overcoming my initial difficulties, I was able to understand and commend the respect that Dr. Uribe holds towards the importance of moral values in the leadership arena—such as honesty, a sense of duty and responsibility, fairness, firmness, and the value of keeping your word to those in leadership. As a consequence, she shows the correlating increase in trust and, consequently, the development of the same values in those who are being directed, managed and organized by management, especially by senior management.

Dr. Uribe's intention is laudable, and I believe deserves to be appreciated and considered, perhaps setting it in proper perspective. I wish to explain my interpretation.

Throughout history and at any latitude and longitude around the world, companies, communities and societies have been built with one common goal: to seek purpose. The military forces of a nation will ensure border security; the country's political and economic structure is set up for the well-being of its citizens; the leadership of a business, company and financial institution will look to do good by creating profits for its employees and shareholders. But the real problem, from my point of view, it is not the structure itself, but the heart of the individual leading the organization.

If those being led have lost confidence in their leaders, it is often due to one thing—greed, plus a good dose of selfishness.

In my view this book—through extensive studies, interviews and positive examples—strives to suggest attitudes and behaviors that help to overcome, and even abandon, the narrow view of momentary personal benefit that a leader can face, in order to acquire a broader good that will benefit more people than only those under the guidance of the leader. In Dr. Uribe's vision, if all leaders took this view—the view of sacrificing personal gain for the benefit of all—the ripple effect would be transformed to exponentially benefit the wider populous for citizens, insitutions, structures and society in general.

I really admire the vision Dr. Uribe has laid out, and gladly encourage reading the book. But I trust that the reader will allow me to expound a little, as a result of my personal experiences, on the soul, the heart of man, to which I referred above.

Every country, every structure, every business and company, small or large, is made up of men and women, and it is true they often have to adjust to create and live by strict rules, standards and morality they adhere to. They are individuals...we are individuals...always building the world around us to make it better or worse.

History teaches that when people with great ideals and good-hearted intentions are leading an organization, their ideals carry them through critical and difficult times that result in a greater good for all. Unfortunately, the opposite is also true.

So what is the solution? What "road" do we take that does *not* take us in the wrong direction in moments of crisis that will lead to failures or worse? For me, the answer is simple: the road that leads to love as understood by the Charity of Our Lord and mentioned throughout the Gospels. If you know and really live as He has taught us, with your primary emphasis on caring for and valuing people, not organizations, then you will be heading in the right direction to really understand and put into practice the principles and practices found in this book.

In closing, I wish to draw the reader to what I feel is the most important meaning found in Dr. Uribe's writing: the positive value of people and their potential for good.

Sincerely,

Mons. Giacomo Pappalardo

The Vatican

#Values

#Values

THE SECRET TO TOP-LEVEL PERFORMANCE IN BUSINESS AND LIFE

Dr. Betty Uribe

NEXT CENTURY

PUBLISHING

#Values
The Secret to Top-Level Performance in Business and Life

Published by Next Century Publishing
Las Vegas, Nevada
www.NextCenturyPublishing.com

ISBN: 978-1-68102-122-5

Printed in the United States of America

DEDICATION

———•———

I dedicate this book to my oldest brother, Alex Fernando Rengifo, who gave me my first scholarship of $500 dollars, at a time in my life when I had only the clothes on my back, and a dream to educate myself so I could make a significant impact in the world, one person at a time. At that time he also quit his job in Northern California and rented an apartment for both of us in San Diego County so I would have a place to live. He taught me to squeeze every inch out of life; to grow tentacles and touch the entire world; to take the essence of life and beauty; to smell the music and taste the colors; to breathe in every second of life, and to give to others with grace, what has been given to me in grace.

Through this work, we will pay forward my brother's gift. My hope is to raise funds to provide 100 scholarships for underserved young adults in each continent; brilliant young minds who are values-based leaders, willing to pay it forward so this legacy will go on around the world for generations to come. I am deeply grateful for the opportunity to honor my brother's legacy with this work.

To my mother Beatriz Montaña de Rengifo who left wealth and comfort in Colombia to give us peace and the freedom to attend church and obtain an education, and to my father Luis Carlos Rengifo, who taught me about values and character, and about paying it forward. To both my parents who taught me about the meaning of life through their prioritized actions, may they both rest in peace, and rejoice in the company of Tio Ismael, Tia Sofia and Tio Gustavo.

To Tia Ruby, uncle Ivan and Tia Rosanna for bringing me to this wonderful country at a young age and for taking me under your wing along with Tia Nohemi and Tia Marta when my parents passed away. Your support, motherly and fatherly love, have been invaluable.

To the values-based leaders in my life who have demonstrated leading with values, integrity, and making a difference in the people they touch for generations to come.

Most important, I dedicate this book to our Heavenly Father, the center of my life. For opening the doors so dignitaries and leaders around the world and students of leadership can read this work and pay it forward.

ACKNOWLEDGMENTS

To my children Kristopher, Alexandria and Sandra, my biggest cheerleaders.

To my firstborn Kristopher for your talented photography, capturing the essence of leaders highlighted herein, and becoming part of this journey in the process.

To Juan Carlos Uribe for your love, insight and wisdom.

To my brothers Carlos, Fernando and Ricardo, for your never-ending encouragement and support.

To my dissertation committee chair Dr. Michelle Rosensitto, Dr. June Schmieder and Judge Tobin, for standing for me to produce a quality dissertation that would add to the body of knowledge, which became the foundation for this book.

To Alex Fortunati, Gregory Jacobson, Lynn Carter, Pablito Schneider, Marietta Nelson, and Michelle Colón-Johnson, who took the time to read the first manuscript and provide insight and feedback that helped shape the final draft.

To Alex for working hard, rushing the Italian translation so the Monsignor could read and recommend this work.

To Gloria Hirson, for your ideas, resources and passion for making a difference.

To Beth Lottig, the best writer and partner through this entire journey; from the moment I laid volumes of research on the table, asking you to turn this dissertation into the framework for a book; the late nights and early mornings, countless interviews, and for sharing in my passion for injecting #Values back into leadership around the globe for generations.

To Myrna Soto, for naming my very first book … #Values! Something we all need in our lives.

To Lydia's Ladies for your prayers and words of encouragement.

To my publisher and the team comprised of Beth, Ken, Shannon, Simon, and Rod, you came to rescue as I expedited the timeline of the book due to my brother's terminal illness. For your passion for making a difference, and for your incredible support and prayers along the way, you have all been a blessing through this process.

I am mostly grateful to God, for His love and wisdom, for expanding my territory and opening doors, showing apostolic favor and grace so this work can reach every corner of the earth at a time when our world and our people need it the most. I am deeply grateful and humbled to be His vessel.

I chose these leaders because they embody the quintessential role models for each of the topics discussed in the chapters.

I chose the broad audience of heads of state, CEOs, and students of leadership because these are the most influential roles in a country's and community's culture. In essence, these roles drive the culture.

Robert E. Bard is the president and CEO of LATINA *Style* Inc. He serves on the Board of Directors of Parents Step Ahead, the advisory boards of HITEC, Women of Alpfa, is the Chairman of ANSO, the Association of Naval Service Officers and serves on the Board of Directors of Score. He and his wife, Ms. Lupita Colmenero, publisher of El Hispano News and Founder of Parents Step Ahead Foundation, live and serve their community in Dallas.

Mr. Andrew Benton has served as the president of Pepperdine University since 2000 and serves as immediate past chair of the Association of Independent California Colleges and Universities. He is on the Boards of Directors of the National Association of Independent Colleges and Universities and the President's Cabinet of the West Coast Conference. A lawyer by training, President Benton cares deeply about his students and is often called "the students' president." Benton currently resides in Malibu with his wife, Debby.

Major General Julie Bentz, PhD is the Vice Director of the Joint Improvised Explosive Device Defeat Organization. As the former Director of the Strategic Capabilities Policy with the National Security Council, Bentz has been responsible for writing presidential policy, coordinating interagency dialogue, informing presidential budgetary decisions and building consensus on interagency initiatives in programs that develop United States Strategic capabilities to meet 21st century requirements.

Vice Admiral Raquel C. Bono of the US Navy currently serves as Director, Defense Health Agency. She has also served as Deputy Director of Medical Resources, Plans and Policy, Chief of Naval Operations, US Pacific Command Surgeon, Acting Commander Joint Task Force of National Capital Region Medical, Director of the National Capital Region Medical Directorate of the Defense Health Agency and as the 11th Chief of Navy Medical Corps. She served in both Operations Desert Shield and Desert Storm as head of casualty receiving. She is the mother of three grown children and resides with her husband in Bethesda, MD.

Darrell Brown is the Senior Vice President of US Bank, the nation's fifth largest commercial bank with over $438 billion in assets and 18.6 million customers. With over forty years of leadership and management roles within the banking industry, he is responsible for strategic, tactical and profit and loss management for close to one hundred retail branch facilities and is the highest ranking African American in Retail Banking. Motivated by a passion for his community, Darrell has dedicated his time to young people and works unceasingly to assist in providing brighter possibilities for their future.

Robert Owen Carr is the founder and CEO of Heartland Payment Systems, a Fortune 1000 company and one of the largest debit and credit card transaction companies in America. Just as important, he earned a national reputation as a trailblazer for ethical reform of the payments industry. Mr. Carr serves on the Board of Trustees at Lewis College in Illinois and is the founder of the Give Something Back Foundation, which provides financial support to college students from poor and working-class backgrounds. He is also the author of *THROUGH THE FIRES: An American Business Story of Turbulence, Triumph and Giving Back* and *Working Class to College: The Promise and Peril for Blue Collar America.*

Lynn Carter is the former president of Capital One Bank. She is an experienced leader who has spent more than forty years in the banking industry with an added focus of building community development expertise. She has been active in business, community and nonprofit organizations, currently serving on the boards of Hiscox Ltd, American Express Centurion Bank, Phoenix House and BankWork$. Most recently, she has served on the boards of the Autry National Center and Operation Hope. She splits her time between California and Connecticut.

 **Alex Fortunati** is the founder and former CEO of one of the largest minority owned facility maintenance companies with a nationwide footprint. He has served on the boards of the American Heart Association of Los Angeles, Pepperdine University, Antioch University Board of Trustees, Hispanic 100, Latin Business Association and Taller San Jose. He was appointed by then California Governor Schwarzenegger to be Commissioner of the State Lottery. Alex and his wife, Susana, live in Orange County, California.

 **Retired US Army Lt. General Mick Kicklighter** served 35 years in the U.S. Army, with two tours of duty in Vietnam. He has commanded at all levels, from Commander of US Army Pacific, to Commander of the 25th Infantry Division, to the Commander of the U.S. Army Security Assistance Command. He also served as the Director of the Army Staff. A highly decorated US Solider, LTG Kicklighter continues to serve the nation in a number of senior positions with the Departments of Defense, State, and Veteran Affairs.

 **David Long** is the Founder and CEO of MyEmployees, as well as a speaker and author of the Wall Street Journal bestselling leadership book, *Built to Lead*. MyEmployees is an organization that shows companies how

to supercharge employee engagement with a vibrant workplace culture, and they practice what we preach. He leads by example and cultivates a culture of growth with his company-wide book clubs. David and his wife Janet reside in Wilmington, NC.

William Michael Reynolds is a platinum business broker of his own real estate company and former CEO and Chairman of Luminart Corporation, a startup oil fuel and construction business company he launched and grew to $25M in revenue in under three years. A seasoned C-level executive, his leadership strengths are rooted in his ability to create strategic alliances, effectively align with key business initiatives and build and retain high-performing teams. A master of M&A and turnarounds, Mr. Reynolds' notable achievements include reverse acquisitions of both Herbalife and PAX TV. He currently lives and works in Peoria, AZ.

Shaheen Sadeghi is the founder and CEO of LAB Holdings (short for Little American Business), a real estate company with a passion for revitalization. With a background in design, Sadeghi is known for creating "anti-malls" and revitalizing downtown Anaheim with the Packing House and Center Street Promenade. He brings his creative touch and leadership values to every endeavor he undertakes. Shaheen and his wife, Linda, reside in Laguna Beach, California.

Major General Angela (Angie) Salinas, US Marine Corps (RET) is known for the stark contrast of her short stature and her commanding presence. As a result of her professional acumen and strong, consistent leadership, she is the first Hispanic woman to become a US Marine Corps general officer, and the sixth woman in the Marine Corps to reach the rank of brigadier general. Major General Salinas retired after thirty-nine years of military service, rising from private to major general. At the time of her retirement in 2013, she was the senior ranking female and Hispanic in the USMC. Salinas currently resides in San Antonio Texas, where she now leads the Girl Scouts of Southwest Texas as CEO.

Maria Salinas is the former Chairwoman of ProAmerica Bank and President & Founder of Salinas Consulting, LLC, a finance and accounting project management firm. An accomplished businesswoman, entrepreneur, CPA and community leader, her business acumen and financial expertise has led her to the boardrooms of community organizations, higher education institutions, and a community bank. Recipient of the 2010 Professional Services Award from the National Latina Business

Women's Association of Los Angeles, Maria and her husband live in Pasadena, California.

Pablo Schneider is the CEO of The Wider Net, a firm dedicated to advancing diverse leaders in top leadership and to helping companies grow in diverse markets. He also serves as a Special Advisor to APCH on building a portfolio of high-growth Minority Business Enterprises. During his twenty-five-year business career, he has served as a senior executive with BlueCross and Blue Shield, Delta Dental, and three growth ventures. He has served on private, non-profit, and governmental boards for the past twenty years. Pablo and his wife, Debby, have five awesome children and are in their 24th year of home-schooling.

Harris H. Simmons is Chairman and CEO of Zions Bancorporation, a $60 billion (assets) bank holding company that operates approximately 450 full-service banking offices throughout the western United States. A native of Salt Lake City, Simmons has served for more than thirty-five years with the organization. Active in community and industry affairs, Simmons has served as chairman or president of the American Bankers Association, Utah Symphony, Utah Foundation, and Economic Development Corporation of Utah, among many other organizational leadership roles. He and his wife, Amanda, live in Salt Lake City, Utah.

 **Matt Toledo** is the CEO of the Los Angeles Business Journal, the largest regional business media company in California. Under his direction, the Los Angeles Business Journal has been recognized as the best regional business journal in the country for its compelling coverage and quality journalism. Toledo is a passionate civic leader, serving on numerous boards as director and advisor, including Pepperdine University, Los Angeles Chamber of Commerce, Los Angeles Economic Development Corporation, the Los Angeles Sports and Entertainment Commission, among many others. Matt resides in Los Angeles, California. Always optimistic about life, he is a devoted father to his two daughters and is a passionate athlete, traveler and foodie.

 **Ash Patel** presently serves as President/ CEO of Commercial Bank of California, and most recently served as Chairman of the Board for National Bank of California. With over twenty years of banking experience, from entrepreneurial orientation to banking with the small businesses, his principle management style is based upon investing in human capital and enhancing customer experience. The hospitality industry has been one of the focal strategies of his success. From lending to consulting with and understanding the nuances of the hospitality industry, his diverse background provides extremely valuable insight to these banking markets..

CONTENTS

#Values

FOREWORD

———•·—·——

The subject of leadership in the context of values—character, ethics, and integrity—could not be more timely. We are living in a world that is becoming increasingly more dangerous and, at the same time, more fragile. Honesty and virtue are at a premium. We need a new generation of leaders who understand and subscribe to the traditional values that made our country great. Dr. Betty Uribe's study of Values-Based Leadership comes at a critical moment.

Dr. Uribe's life is a classic American story of dedication, caring, sacrifice, hard work, and leadership. She has climbed the corporate ladder and the academic ladder, and has reached the top of both—all while taking care of a family, sometimes as a single mom. She learned and honed her leadership style and skills first in the corporate trenches and then expanded and contextualized them in the academic classroom. Betty has offered us a glimpse into her fascinating journey, first with her doctoral thesis at Pepperdine University and now in this book.

In his book *Discover Your True North*, Bill George quotes John Donahoe (former president and CEO of eBay) as having said: "Leadership is a journey, not a destination." Betty's book, *#Values: The Secret to Top Level Performance in Business and Life,* clearly illustrates the truth of that observation as she records the milestones of her own leadership journey in business and life. She deftly blends academic models with both her own experience and the personal reminiscences of men and women she regards as exemplars of the many and varied styles of effective leadership. The unifying principle on the broad spectrum of leadership types she explores is the importance of values.

I would add just a few words to Mr. Donahoe's idea: Leadership is a journey *that never ends*. Good leaders continue to learn and improve throughout the great trek. *#Values* is an enjoyable read. It is also thoughtful and provocative. The principles considered are worthy of deep pondering, self-examination, and reflection. Journey on.

Mick Kicklighter

Lt. General, US Army (Retired)

★ ★ ★

PREFACE

---•---

"Personal leadership is the process of keeping your vision and values before you and aligning your life to be congruent with them."
—Stephen Covey

When I presented my doctoral dissertation on Values-Based Leadership in July of 2012, I could never have imagined how its contents would ultimately transform my life. I was simply driven by the idea that leading with values at the center of one's organization was key to overall success.

Having two daughters in high school in Southern California at the time and a son starting a business in Colorado, I wanted to make sure they—and other young people in America and around the world—would have role models to look up to and emulate. I am grateful to the wonderful leaders who took part in this study for the experiences and wisdom they shared, which added so much richness to my own story. They afforded me the opportunity to dig deep into their lives and leadership journeys so others could gain insight into what it takes to be a values-based leader. I wanted to find those role models and highlight them in a way that would inspire others who could affect positive change in their own spheres of influence.

That is what this book is all about.

The research and data collected in my doctoral dissertation are the backbone of the book you hold in your hands right now. What I discovered in my research is a game-changer: Those who are able to weather financial downturns, fiscal stress, and other obstacles—that could crumble their organization, their community and their industry—are those whose values of honesty, integrity, courage, responsibility, family, wisdom, and leading with a higher purpose are at the core of their leadership style and decision-making. Bottom line? Alignment of values in leadership matters more than you can imagine. Living your values is the key to top-level performance in business and in life.

I have a passion to make an impact on a global scale. Yes, that is a lofty goal, but I truly believe that great things can be accomplished with hard work and resolute determination. In the words of Malcolm Gladwell in his book, *The Tipping Point: How Little Things Can Make a Big Difference*:

> "The tipping point is that magic moment when an idea, trend, or social behavior crosses a threshold, tips, and spreads like wildfire."

Through this book, I want to create a **social epidemic of values-based leadership** in business and in life. Our values should not change when we leave the workplace; they should encompass our personal and professional lives, always aligned and at the core of every decision, every action, every relationship, every conversation. We should embrace our values in all parts of our lives... It's up to us.

By creating a legacy of values-based leaders who are inspired to encourage and develop other values-based leaders, we will be impacting the next generation by building trust, value, and leading from a place of integrity.

We will create a tipping point for the idea of values-based leadership in our personal and professional lives that will *spread like wildfire.*

I've said for years now that I want to inject values back into the world. I may be an ordinary person, but one with a strong voice, the right drive, and a passionate belief that I *can* make an extraordinary impact on the world, one conversation at a time. Through the pages of this book, I wish to inspire you to believe that you can make a difference as well—as you commit to living and leading with the right set of core values that will set a social epidemic in motion.

CHAPTER ONE

Life and Leadership Values

Values-based leaders share common foundational values – your values determine your success!

"Values are and should be the ultimate test in any situation or choice in life."
—Peter Drucker

It was around the end of 2007 when the economy began to fall in the United States. All of a sudden, the news was flooded with stories of leaders who were once role models in every area of life, but this time, these leaders kep falling and the news continued to be flooded with the unfortunate stories. I noticed a common thread amongst these leaders: The decisions they were making in their personal and business lives were not aligned with who they were—or at least with the image they portrayed of themselves.

So I asked myself, *"Why is it that some leaders rise to the very top and become role models, yet suddenly we see them making headlines and hitting rock bottom as a result of a wrong decision or action, which then affected their community, their companies, and ultimately their families?"*

As I pondered this question, something perhaps bigger began to emerge: there appeared to be few leaders left who *led with their values, leading* with integrity, making decisions according to their values, leading high-performing organizations, and always focusing on the good of the whole.

I chose to study three different arenas: top-level generals in all areas of the military, CEOs of entrepreneurial organizations, and C-level executives in finance.

Why these three areas of study?

It's simple. When you think of times in history when a new country was born or rebuilt anywhere in the world, it was these three areas that took a front seat in bringing order, building the culture, and ensuring the financial vibrancy and economic livelihood of a country, a village, a community, and our world as we know it.

Today I interviewed one of the greatest leaders in the financial services industry: Harris Simmons, Chairman and Chief Executive Officer at Zions Bancorporation. He said, "Banking is like oxygen; everyone takes it for granted until it's not there. Finance is the economic oxygen for the world." As I ponder Harris Simmons' words, I'd like to think of values in the same way. You don't know they are there until they are gone. All of a sudden, there is a spotlight placed on the situation, the people, the organization, the government, the country.

It is important to note that the leaders highlighted in this book have proven that it is possible (and essential) to lead a values-centered life without sacrificing top-line revenue growth and sustainable top results in the journey.

In 2012, the news media was bombarded by scandalous headlines of US Secret Service agents who had been involved with a slew of call girls while the US President visited another country. Their values were undoubtedly far from their minds when they chose to entertain these women, particularly because there were legitimate concerns that they had planted bugs, disabled weapons, or possibly jeopardized the security of the president or the country. This is only one example of thousands of headlines depicting role models (and sometimes also their teams) making decisions that led to their ultimate fall, losing face and trust with their countries, communities, organizations, and finally their own families. We have seen international role models lose everything because they made a bad decision, or worse, they rationalized a bad decision and later tried to explain it away instead of owning the fact that they made a mistake.

For the purpose of this book I have defined values-based leaders as *leaders whose actions are congruent with their espoused values, leading with integrity, focusing on the good of the whole, and making a positive impact on others.* They think, talk, and feel strongly about their values. Let me take this definition a little deeper:

> **Congruency**: When we have congruency, our actions align with our words; there are no guessing games and those around us know what to expect from us.

Integrity: Integrity goes deeper than just telling the truth. I often tell my leadership team that "integrity happens when no one is looking." It is about standing for what you believe, even when those around you are against you.

Focusing on the good of the whole: This means taking your eye off yourself and putting your focus on the country, the organization, or the team, rather than self-gain. It is understanding the long-term implications of a decision.

Making a positive impact in others: Making a positive impact means always "looking out" and asking yourself *how you can make a difference for those around you* and how you can inspire them to pay it forward.

I remember years ago when my father passed away. My brothers asked that I take over the family business; it was a transportation business in Colombia, South America. I was a Senior Manager at Wells Fargo at that time, responsible for strategy for 300 branches in Southern California. I thought to myself: "How am I going to do this?" I decided to allow a relative to watch over the business; after all, my father had sold most of the business by the time he became very ill, and I didn't think it would be too much of a burden to run a South American business from North America. To my surprise, after one year I flew to Bogotá, Colombia, only to find out that the company was now in serious debt and many people had not been paid. I was devastated to see my father's good name being dragged through the mud in that way after he had worked his entire life with a high level of integrity. I wanted to restore my father's good name, so I traveled around and shook hands personally with all the debtors telling them, "My name is Betty Rengifo. I am Luis Carlos Rengifo's daughter; you are now doing business with me as if I were my own father. On my father's honor, I promise to pay you every penny myself." It took me over two years to pay the debt from my personal finances. Once all the debt was paid, I sold the remainder of the company. Though I could have left the company to go into bankruptcy and not taken personal responsibility for a debt that was not technically mine to pay, I chose to do the right thing. No, it was not easy. I was a woman in a man's world, enduring something bigger than myself, yet I knew the right thing was to serve the family honor, restore my family's name, and live by "the code," like an armor. I needed to lead with integrity through actions that were congruent with my espoused values, focusing on the good of the whole, and making a positive impact in others.

Many times in life we are called to do something bigger than us; we are called to make decisions, and often we come to a fork in the road that requires a judgment call. As I said earlier, "Integrity happens when no one is looking." Andy, one of my mentors and my chosen brother today, said to me a long time ago: "People show their true colors when they are in crisis; sit down and take a front-row seat to their values." When you do the right thing, the right things happen. In order to achieve high-level performance in business and life, we must choose to do the right thing—sometimes the hard thing—over and over again.

Values, Attitudes, and Needs

Milton Rokeach was one of the earliest researchers who did much to advance the study of values. According to Rokeach (1973), the function of values is to guide our thoughts and actions, to satisfy our needs, and ultimately to regard ourselves and to be regarded by others as the social definition of morality and competence. This is particularly critical in top leadership positions, as a company's or a country's vision and mission define their values. When an executive does not act according to the company's vision and mission, they risk losing the trust of their constituents, and a vacuum is formed, much like we saw in the mortgage industry not too long ago. Communication is scarce as the leaders try to figure out what to release to the public and their employees. This vacuum literally sucks the energy out of a company and its employees. Morale is affected, and all of a sudden productivity suffers, and eventually the company's bottom line.

According to Rokeach, the root of a person's values is his or her personal needs. Like Maslow's hierarchy of needs (see Figure 1), basic needs must be satisfied in order for an individual to grow into the next stage of development.

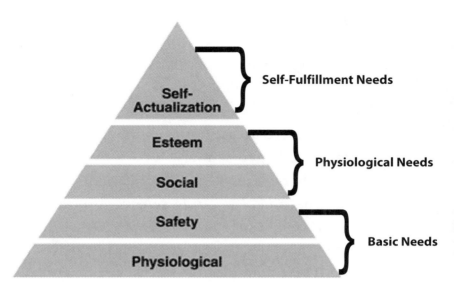

Figure 1: Maslow's Hierarchy of Needs

Once a person is able to take care of their primary needs, he or she rises to the next level, self-esteem, and finally arrives at self-actualization. This, according to Abraham Maslow, is where morality, creativity, spontaneity, problem solving, lack of prejudice, and acceptance of facts occurs. Ram Charan[1] has a similar model he employs for business. This model underscores the importance of senior leadership being visible during times of fiscal stress, at which time leaders must emphasize safety and security, which are critical for people to be free to innovate, produce, problem solve, and accept the facts. You can read about Ram Charan's model in his book *Leadership in the Era of Economic Uncertainty*.

---

[1]   Charan, R. (2009). Leadership in the era of economic uncertainty: The new rules for getting the right things done in difficult times. New York, NY: McGraw Hill.

Rokeach's work was expanded by Schwartz in his article, "Toward a universal psychological structure of human values" in the *Journal of Personality and Social Psychology*. Schwartz and Bilsky defined values as an intersection of goals, hierarchically arranged motivations, and interests. They believed that there are five features common to all definitions of values; according to Schwartz, values are "(1) concepts or beliefs, (2) about desirable states of behaviors, (3) transcend specific situations, (4) guide selection or evaluation of behavior or events, and (5) are ordered by relative importance. The ranking of values, then, is an accurate method to determine a person's driving principles, their transformation of beliefs into action, and their overall motivation as a leader.

How does all of that academic rhetoric on values and doctoral research intersect with real-life application?

It begins in our everyday lives through *our* beliefs, actions, and choices. When you think of someone you trust, most likely they live and lead according to their values. Two popular examples come to mind: *Martin Luther King Jr.*, whose actions showed his commitment to the good of the whole and to bettering the economic and social lives of a specific segment of the population, and *Mother Teresa*, a woman who led with integrity, focusing on the good of mankind and making a positive impact in others. Though it behooves a morally based public figure such as Martin Luther King, Jr. or Mother Teresa to lead with values, examples of values-based leaders can be found in many different sectors of leadership, from the military to the business world and beyond.

When I visited a series of schools in Kenya, Africa—where I have been donating (personally and from speaking engagements) to a few villages so their youth can attend high school—one particular school stood out in the Lila community. When I walked into this school, I saw their values written on every classroom wall; they were in every office, along the paths of the classroom, and embodied in every teacher and every student. I was so impressed when I was told that the girls in the school treasured education so much that they formed a committee to ask the administration to allow them to wake up at 4:30 a.m. so they could begin their studies at 5:30 a.m. and take advantage of that one extra hour of studies. When I asked why in the world they would want to wake up at 4:30 a.m. and start school at 5:30 a.m. (they were already studying until 6:00 p.m. Monday through Saturday), the students told me they realized that they only had four years to get as much education as they could before taking off to the university. I got to sit and talk with four learners (that's what they call their students and teachers—notice they don't differentiate, as this nomenclature applies to everyone in the school); some were high school seniors and others were sophomores. Two of these learners said, "I am going to be a neurosurgeon." One said she is going to be a pilot, another a news reporter, and the last one is going to be a judge. There was no hesitation in their statements. They knew, beyond a shadow of a doubt, what they were going to study. What are the chances that four randomly selected high school students would have the drive and certainty that these students showed? This is an example of what can be seen when leaders lead with values. I can personally say there is no one in that school who does not embrace the values that are stated on the walls: *Be your best, you can do anything, give unconditionally,* among others. Values indeed correlate to success for those learners, and they correlate to success for us as well.

Pinpointing that correlation was the purpose of my study, and the ranking of values, among other factors, was the method I chose to use in my research. I believed that if I could find a correlation in the values ranking of successful leaders I would be able to prove that leading with values leads to success.

Does this kind of values-based leadership apply to all studies, pursuits, careers, and lifestyles? In short, yes. In their book *The Art of Command*, Laver and Matthews cite General Puller as a values-based leader. He was also known as the hero of the U.S. Marine Corps. Puller inspired and influenced others by always looking out for the well-being of his subordinates, giving his best, leading from the front lines, and keeping a close personal connection with his people. Herbert Kelleher, founder and former CEO of Southwest Airlines, is another leader who has been acknowledged for his integrity. He makes a positive impact on his employees and leads with a servant heart, focusing on the good of the whole. Kelleher's company has been profitable for more than thirty-eight consecutive years, has never furloughed an employee, and at the time of this writing carries the most originating domestic passengers of any US airline. Southwest Airlines is the only airline to make *Fortune's* top ten list of the world's Most Admired Companies. Kelleher himself has received numerous awards and honors, including the U.S. Chamber Business Leadership Hall of Fame, CEO of the Year, and is one of history's top three CEOs according to *Chief Executive* magazine, among other honors. Kelleher successfully translated nearly forty years of values-based leadership into a life well lived that has impacted countless others beyond the walls of his office.

> MY TEAMS HAVE PROVEN TIME AND AGAIN THAT VALUES PLAY A CRITICAL ROLE FOR SUSTAINABLE SUCCESS IN BUSINESS AND IN LIFE.

His values, realized in his actions, led to his personal and career success.

Values-centered leadership produces results that propel an organization to the top of their market. Values-based living elevates life itself from merely getting by, to creating a lasting impact that replicates in the lives of multitudes.

I have personally seen this play out in my own experience, while doing turnarounds in the last two decades for three different financial services institutions...based on values. My teams have proven time and again that VALUES play a critical role for sustainable success in business and in life.

I am proud to say that even after I left each bank to move on to the next turnaround, the organizations I assisted remain in the top of their markets to this day. Those results speak for themselves. Like Kelleher of Southwest and so many others, I believe—and have seen the proof—that leading with values shapes organizational culture in a positive way.

I was fortunate to learn *character* from my father and *values* from my mother, and for both I am eternally grateful. After living according to my values, and now having studied values for such a long time, I see values and character are interchangeable, as you can't have one without the other.

Because of my parents, I have been witness to the power of values-based living. My life took a dramatic turn at the age of twelve when I chose to leave behind the comfort and financial security of my father's home in Colombia for the unknown in North America. My mother modeled values-based living for me as she valued and served everyone around her, regardless of their station in life. I, in turn, modeled living with values to my own children in order to pass on the legacy my father and mother left me. I was given the gift of discovering how much my values impacted my daughter Sandra when she began her university studies; she wrote me a letter that I will never forget. She thanked me for the sacrifices I made and the values I modeled in order that she might have the opportunity to make an impact in the world in her own way. As a parent, I can't imagine anything more poignant than hearing those words from my own child. I cannot read it without emotions brimming to the surface.

I am reminded every time I read that letter that the values I strive to build in my organizations and uphold in my life are not some pie-in-the-sky ideological notion. They are the oxygen, the feet, the arms, and the backbone of everything I am and everything I believe. Whether you realize it or not, your values are of vital significance to your life and legacy. With that in mind, it is important to evaluate and fully understand your values in their most uncontrived form. That is where the research of Milton Rokeach comes into our study of values.

The Basics of Values

According to Rokeach's *The Nature of Human Values*, the consistently occurring values in his survey have been confirmed through decades of research and hundreds of cross-cultural studies. The behaviors of leaders are determined by the relative importance they place on a particular value. Therefore, the actions that leaders take are linked with their values and can be observed through their decisions as well as their demonstrated priorities and actions.

As leaders we need to look to a leadership model that will both produce growth personally and professionally—the future profitability and sustainability of our organizations absolutely depend upon it. In addition, we need to evaluate how we, as members of a local and global community, can effectively model living with values so that we can make a difference in this world. It's time to stop settling for the status quo and to reach for our true potential as top-level leaders and influencers.

> THE ACTIONS THAT LEADERS TAKE ARE LINKED WITH THEIR VALUES AND CAN BE OBSERVED THROUGH THEIR DECISIONS AS WELL AS THEIR DEMONSTRATED PRIORITIES AND ACTIONS.

Built upon over 200 years of reliance on the excellence and integrity of leadership, the military puts high emphasis on the actions of its leaders and trains each individual for a high level of performance. As Frances Hesselbein states in *Be, Know, Do: Leadership the Army Way*, the competence of character is a key component of the expectations for military leadership. Since individual values have been linked to military and corporate leaders' ability to create culture, it is important to understand how senior leaders in finance, the military, and entrepreneurial organizations shape their cultures. My doctoral dissertation study explored just that: how senior executives utilize their values and leadership characteristics to affect corporate culture and performance.

QUESTIONS TO KEEP YOU THINKING

Note: Throughout the book, I have incorporated these question sections to stimulate further thought and self-examination. Because this book is designed so each chapter can be read as a standalone vignette, it is not necessary to read the chapters in a linear fashion. The questions at the end are meant to stimulate thought and reaction, not to put a plan together. I plan to provide more actionable items in my forthcoming field book on values, which I discuss at the end of this book.

Take a moment to evaluate the following terminal and instrumental values, as the study participants did, ranking each value from one to eighteen. Each value is accompanied by a short description and a blank space. Study each list and think of how much each value may act as a guiding principle in your life. To begin, select the value that is of most importance to you. Write the number 1 in the blank space next to that value. Next, choose the value that is of second in importance to you and write the number 2 in the blank next to it. Work your way through the list until you have ranked all 18 values on this page. When ranking, take your time and think carefully. Feel free to go back and change your order, should you have second thoughts about any of your answers. When you have completed the ranking of both sets of values, the result should represent an accurate picture of how you really feel about what's important in your life.

Rokeach Terminal Values: The Goals You Would Like to Have Achieved at the End of Your Lifetime

___ A comfortable life (a prosperous life)

___ Equality (brotherhood and equal opportunity for all)

___ An exciting life (a stimulating, active life)

___ Family security (taking care of loved ones)

___ Freedom (independence and free choice)

___ Health (physical and mental well-being)

___ Inner harmony (freedom from inner conflict)

___ Mature love (sexual and spiritual intimacy)

___ National security (protection from attack)

___ Pleasure (an enjoyable, leisurely life)

___ Salvation (saved, eternal life)

___ Self-respect (self-esteem)

___ A sense of accomplishment (lasting contribution)

___ Social recognition (respect and admiration)

___ True friendship (close companionship)

___ Wisdom (a mature understanding of life)

___ A world at peace (a world free of war and conflict)

___ A world of beauty (beauty of nature and the arts)

Rokeach Instrumental Values: Values Utilized Along Your Leadership Journey

(Means to Achieve Your Terminal Values)

___ Ambitious (Hard-working, aspiring)

___ Broad-minded (Open-minded)

___ Capable (Competent, effective)

___ Clean (Neat, tidy)

___ Courageous (Standing up for your belief)

___ Forgiving (Willing to pardon others)

___ Helpful (Working for the welfare of others)

___ Honest (Sincere, truthful)

___ Imaginative (daring, creative)

___ Independent (Self-reliant, self-sufficient)

___ Intellectual (Intelligent, reflective)

___ Logical (Consistent, rational)

___ Loving (Affectionate, tender)

___ Loyal (Faithful to friends or the group)

___ Obedient (Dutiful, respectful)

___ Polite (Courteous, well-mannered)

___ Responsible (Dependable, reliable)

___ Self-controlled (Restrained, self-disciplined)

If you've completed your terminal and instrumental values rankings, you may now compare them with the rankings of the high-level senior executives and military generals in the study.

Top Terminal and Instrumental Values

After surveying the high-level participants in the study, the top five *terminal* values (what they would like at the end of their life) were **family, health, spirituality, wisdom,** and **freedom.**

The top five *instrumental* values (those they use along their leadership journey) were **honesty, courage, being responsible, helpful**, and **loving**.

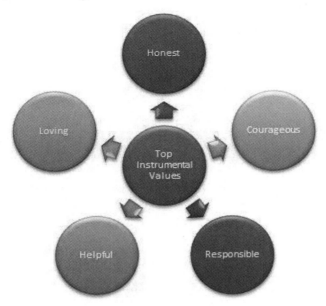

All the leaders in the study led with a higher purpose. When asked, each of them felt they were leading for a purpose that was "bigger than themselves." This was a key finding, as in times of fiscal stress, the leaders always turned for the main reason they lead in the first place, connected with that higher purpose, and made decisions based on that.

Being a Great Follower is Important

It is also important to note that all the leaders in the study made it a point to talk about their desire to not only be great leaders, but also *great followers*. The intrinsic nature of the values these leaders espoused—honesty, courage, being responsible, helpful, and loving—made them good followers. They were also teachable, not only allowing but also welcoming others to provide honest, courageous feedback. In my career I find a few leaders with this specific characteristic. Most leaders think they have to have the answer and many are not open to feedback. This is an area where experienced, successful leaders set themselves apart from others who might not have the experience or self-assurance. A great example of this is the downturn of the economy, after which it was found that the employees knew the issues all along, but their leaders did not listen.

Top Instrumental Values *– Those Used Along One's Leadership Journey*

In their 2002 book *The Leadership Challenge*, Kouzes and Posner surveyed over 75,000 people around the world. When asked what they value most about a leader people are willing to follow, more than 50 percent of votes were given to the following characteristics: Honesty, Competence, Forward-looking, and Inspirational. When looking further into the analysis, nearly 90 percent of constituents want their leaders to be honest above all else. Honesty is the foundation of trust, so it is no wonder that it showed up as the top instrumental value of my study participants. Honesty creates integrity within self, alignment (congruency) of values and actions, with no compromise. In my interview with CEO Harris Simmons, he shared that *intellectual honesty* was one of his most highly valued characteristics. It was really interesting talking with Harris, because his perspective is deeper than most. In his version of honesty, you don't rationalize the truth:

"At one level, honesty is truth. Intellectual honesty is being honest with yourself, not rationalizing your way to a decision, thinking through things, and being willing to say what is true, even when it's inconvenient. It's not just about what's good for me. It's about the good of the whole."

This kind of honesty evaluates what is best for the good of the whole, something that defines the values-based leaders in my study.

It is also noteworthy that the top five instrumental values were *intrinsic* in nature, or those that are inherently rewarding to pursue for its own sake. In contrast, the following lowest-ranked bottom values were extrinsic in nature (value assigned by external factors): social recognition, a world of beauty, being self-controlled, clean, and obedient. These extrinsic values are centered more on external approval or reward. While these instrumental values are certainly important to uphold and are worthy of attention, they were the lowest ranked by the participants when considering values that shape one's journey in leadership and in life.

It is also worth noting that the top five instrumental values of the study participants did *not* include *ambitious, intellectual, independent, logical,* or *capable.* These values, though characteristic of many top CEOs, executives, and other generally successful people, were not what the group of leaders in my study chose as their top five. The values they chose to be representative of their "behavioral means for achieving an end goal" remarkably centered on *intrinsic* value to others: honest, courageous, responsible, helpful, and loving.

Founder and CEO of LAB Holdings (short for Little American Business) Shaheen Sadeghi, whom I had the honor to interview for this book after he received the highest honor as an entrepreneur by the Orange County Business Journal in 2015, echoed my study results as he listed his top values: *people, feelings, human touch, understanding people's needs, listening, connection, and a responsibility to listen to the rhythm of your people and put a melody to it.*

> **LEADING AND LIVING BY YOUR VALUES POSITIONS YOU FOR SUCCESSFUL RELATIONSHIPS WITH YOUR TEAM, YOUR COLLEAGUES, YOUR COMMUNITY, YOUR FAMILY, AND YOUR FRIENDS .**

I love that last line. When you lead and live with values, you are able to tap into the underlying rhythm of the people around you. They can align with your melody—your instrumental values, those qualities that shape you—to create a beautiful symphony of generating value for others, positively impacting change, and finding purpose in life. His value of listening to others echoes the findings of my study—that successful, values-based leaders listen to and continuously validate their people. Even when doing a photo shoot for this book, Shaheen insisted that his number two person in the company be in the picture with him. This was very refreshing to see.

Shaheen's right hand and Director of Development Chris Bennett also focuses on understanding employees' individual's genius with—which is normally what they love to do. He matches that with their job description. This is the "secret sauce" of the level of creativity one senses when entering in to the headquarters of LAB Holdings in Irvine, California.

Values clearly play a critical role in success. Something that both Dr. Benton, President of Pepperdine University, and CEO Sadeghi mentioned, is that leading and living with your values positions you for successful relationships with your team, your colleagues, your community, your family, and your friends. When speaking to groups, I like to remind people that there is no such thing as a neutral touch; every touch either adds or depletes value. People who lead and live with values make sure that they are adding value to everyone around them, impacting positive change far beyond the interaction.

Top Terminal Values —*Those a Person Holds at the End of Their Life*

When talking to Zeidy Ballar Gomez, RN BSN, an experienced hospice nurse, about what her patients hold as most important on their death bed, she says, "*Rarely do I hear a person wishing that they had accumulated more possessions or made more money; they wish they had taken more time with their loved ones; it's usually all about quality of life and having taken more risks sooner. You want your loved ones by your side and you want to be touched and loved. It's all about being deeply connected; there's a deep gratitude for others and connection with others.*" I will never forget the words of my very first mentor Tom Timmons; at the time he was the CEO of a local bank in El Toro, California, and I was the branch manager of the local Wells Fargo branch in the same town. Tom said, while addressing a team of bankers I managed at the time, "*When I'm on my death bed, it won't matter how much money or how many titles I've acquired; what will matter is how many people I've touched along the way and the people who are there with me at the end.*"

The top terminal values of the study participants were **family, health, spirituality, wisdom,** and **freedom.** The highest-ranking terminal value of the C-level senior executives interviewed in the study was "family." Does that surprise you? It certainly wouldn't surprise Lynn Carter, president of Capital One Bank from 2007 to 2011. Her stellar career, which spans more than thirty-eight years in the banking industry, and extensive banking and community development expertise, has been a virtual highlight reel of measurable growth. Under Carter's leadership, Capital One grew through a dedicated focus on business and consumer customers, innovative programs, and key strategic acquisitions, with a team of veteran bankers who delivered on strategy that starts with the customer, is supported by strong products, and built on a foundation of financial strength. This was after successfully leading the turnaround of the biggest retail division at Wells Fargo and doing the same at Bank of America. Yet her foundation began long before she stepped into the financial sector as president of one of the largest banks in America. Her family, particularly her grandfather, made an indelible mark on her in her formative years. She related a story during her interview that highlights the influence family had on her:

> As a young girl, I spent my summer with my grandparents and went to the bank regularly with my grandfather. At the particular bank was a man named Mr. Smith, who listened, was responsive, really knew his stuff, and truly took a personal interest in my grandfather's situation and his needs. He took time to build trust with my grandfather. Watching that interaction between my grandfather and Mr. Smith

had such an impact on me as a child. I saw values being modeled right before my eyes during each visit. This time with my grandparents had an incredible influence on me, especially since my mother was a single mom.

When conducting one-on-one meetings with her staff, she showed she truly cared for them and their families. One individual on her senior management team mentioned how *"Lynn made sure I was doing well in my personal relationship; she even offered to have me work close to my loved ones when they were away; she always made sure I was in close contact with them."* From a very young age, Lynn Carter understood the importance of family as an integral part of her leadership style, and she carried that into her career with significant, measurable results. Her people knew beyond a shadow of a doubt that she truly cared about them as people, and that translated to unprecedented results.

Another study participant, Raquel C. Bono, is a vice admiral in the Medical Corps and US Navy Command surgeon with more than thirty-three years as a navy officer. She was the oldest of four children, and her father taught her to be a leader. And that oftentimes meant putting others before herself. She shared a story during our interview that was very revealing of her values:

One time it was 4:00 am and I had a terrible cough. I knew I had promised a young corpsman that I would be there for her when she left on her flight that morning. Though I felt terrible and my husband told me to stay in bed, I got dressed in my uniform so they could spot me and headed to the airport. When I arrived, there she was with her family in tow, getting ready to go through security. She spotted me and called out as she ran to me, "See, I told you my CO was going to be here!" My husband later asked why I did that. I told him, "I did it because I'm asking them to put so much on the line. They're going to a strange country, and the very least I can do is tell them I'm going to take care of their families."

That is the picture of values in action.

QUESTIONS TO KEEP YOU THINKING

1. What are your top five terminal and instrumental values?

2. How do you practice these values in your everyday personal and professional life?

3. Is there any one area where you are currently not aligned with your values?

4. What specific action will you take to ensure your espoused values are congruent with your practiced values?

The actions of values-based leaders are congruent with their espoused value of integrity. They focus on the good of the whole, and make a positive impact in others. They provide living proof that leading with values can impact organizational culture in a positive way. When a leader's actions are congruent with his/her espoused values, it builds a foundation of trust with community leaders, boards of directors, employees, subordinates, and anyone else they touch in their personal and professional lives. Bridging the gap between espoused and practiced values satisfies a critical component in building high-performing organizations that will be sustainable over time.

This is true in both leadership and in life.

As leaders, it behooves us to align our actions with our values and not settle for short-term gains. The first step is getting clear on your values, and the second is following them without exception. It is something very simple as an idea; however, executing on this idea consistently is the key to sustainable success. Those terminal values of family, health, spirituality, wisdom, and freedom come to those who lead with integrity and focus on long-term gain.

CHAPTER SUMMARY – Key Takeaways

* Leaders must be clear on their values and live by them.

* Values-based leaders consistently behave with values at the center of their lives and leadership journey.

* The top five terminal values of values-centered leaders are family, health, spirituality, wisdom, and freedom.

* The top five instrumental values are honesty, courage, being responsible, helpful, and loving.

* All leaders in the study led with a higher purpose, suggesting this purpose is what carried them and their employees through the tough times.

* All leaders in the study welcome feedback from their employees; they are also great followers.

* Leading with values shapes organizational culture in a positive way.

* When leaders are congruent (their actions align with their values), they are able to create a culture that promotes high-performing, sustainable organizations.

CHAPTER TWO

Evaluating Strengths

Those who lead and live with values share common strengths.

"Success is achieved by developing our strengths, not by eliminating our weaknesses."
—Marilyn vos Savant

Strengths play a key role in effective leadership and achieving sustainable top-level performance. It is critical for leaders to know their own strengths as well as those of their people in order to build on the collaborative strength of the team for sustainable results. As vos Savant so eloquently and simply explains, we can never eliminate our weaknesses, yet we can identify and develop our innate strengths.

Many years ago while leading strategy for 300 branches at Wells Fargo, I was introduced to Marcus Buckingham, creator of the Strengthsfinder assessment. Our company invited him to speak to over 1,000 of our management team. Buckingham spoke about creating high performing teams using strength-based leadership. I was so fascinated by the topic that I became certified by the Gallup Organization as a facilitator of their Strengthsfinder process for maximizing strengths and creating high performing leadership teams.

It was then that I understood the power of utilizing my strengths, and the double-edge sword of those strengths, as well as that of those around me. I have embodied strength-based leadership ever since, with sustainable top-level results.

Have you ever been working on something for hours and it seemed like minutes? Have you been told lately: "How do you do that?" to something that comes so naturally to you, you think everyone could do it, and yet others tell you that you are a "natural" at it. In his book, *Good to Great*, Jim Collins talks about the intersection between what we 1) love to do, 2) are best-in-class at, and 3) can make money doing.

Collins calls this the "Hedgehog" and points out that our Hedgehog is our "sweet spot" and as long as we stay within it, the roles we play will seem natural and the throughput will be exponential. You cannot know what you are good at unless you evaluate your strengths; this is what Marcus Buckingham calls your Unique Ability. I call that *Your Genius*—the center point of what you love to do, what you're best in class at, and the passion that drives you.

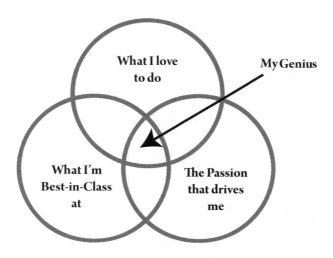

My son Kristopher has always been intelligent and articulate, so when he chose to pursue law school at Chapman University after studying political science as an undergrad, I was not surprised. He secured an internship one summer before law school at a local Los Angeles firm. Everything in his life seemed on course, until he didn't go to law school in the fall. "Why isn't he in school?" I wondered. When asked about it, he responded, "Next semester." *What was I missing?* I finally asked him: *"Do you want to go to law school?"* The answer was no. Honestly, I was a bit shocked, but I have always told my children about their "hedgehog" and encouraged them to pursue their passion. *"Well, what do you want to do?"* I asked, and he thoughtfully replied that he had come to have a passion for photography on our trips abroad in India and Italy. He loved capturing the beauty and grandeur and artistic expression all around him. Though I was worried about him being able to support himself at first, I encouraged him, "If you have a passion for photography, then be the absolute best photographer you can be." He has taken that advice to heart, as he practices architectural and sports photography and can boast numerous magazine covers to affirm his skill and marketability. Just recently he asked me, "Do you remember talking to me about my hedgehog? This is it. I love what I do, and I can create something spectacular, which is a great reward for my work."

I remember, son, and I am so glad you found your passion and so proud of what you've created!

Most high-level leaders recognize that identifying their strengths is absolutely crucial, yet we are often not the best judge of our own key strengths. Since Gallup released the results of its thirty years of research on strengths in the 2001 book by Tom Rath and Marcus Buckingham, *Now, Discover Your Strengths*, more than seven million people have used the StrengthsFinder assessment tools to identify their core strengths. The book spent more than five years on the bestseller lists and ignited a global conversation. Over a decade later, the revised version, StrengthsFinder 2.0, still tops the bestseller lists and continues to uncover how they can "have the opportunity to do what you do best every day." The original book provides great insight from an employer and employee perspective.

We all want to do *what we do best* every day, don't we?

One of my top strengths is that of a Maximizer. People with this strength love to transform something good into something superb. We have little tolerance for mediocrity and like to focus on maximizing people's strengths. Being a maximizer makes me great at turnarounds. I remember how excited I was to rebuild my first engine, *by myself* at the age of nineteen. I often share a picture where I was changing the brakes in my car. I've rebuilt every house

I've ever owned. I love the thrill of taking a non-performing or low-performing organization, and transforming it into something superb. When performing a turnaround, I utilize my own personal strengths, leveraging them with the strengths of my team, for maximum, sustainable results.

To significantly increase throughput, I match people's *genius* to their job; once this happens, a person will never work a day in their life because work feels like a hobby. In order to do this effectively, and as part of building a high-performing team, I ask my leadership team to take the StrengthsFinder test. Anyone can take the StrengthFinder's simple, 20-minute test by purchasing the book and logging into the Gallup website, inserting the secret code found in the book, and following the directions for the online test. It is important that everyone on the team understands one another's strengths, and also the double edge sword of their strength—that sometimes the very strengths of a leader can become weaknesses if not managed effectively. For example, as a Maximizer, I focus on maximizing the strength of the person by continuously coaching that person to their strengths. Someone who doesn't understand that about me could misinterpret my coaching and feel like they can never be good enough. As I write this, I remember my conversations with my father, when I often felt like nothing was ever good enough for him; he always found something that I could do better. Little did I know, my father was also a Maximizer.

There is indeed something to be said for discovering your strengths and utilizing them in your career and in your personal life. There is a certain satisfaction and fulfillment that comes from doing what you were made to do.

It's finding your *genius*.

The Strengthsfinder instrument assesses individuals' unique abilities—leadership competencies—from the positive psychology perspective and measures thirty-four strengths possessed by most leaders. The results from the test taken using the book only yield the top five strengths of an individual. The theory is that we should focus on maximizing our strengths, rather than minimizing our weaknesses. More on this later.

During my research, I sought to discover the top leadership strengths of the leaders in my study utilizing the Strengthsfinder assessment. The results came in and, as I already suspected, similar strengths emerged across the CEOs and C-level executives in business and finance, and military generals.

Top Strengths of Values-Based Leaders

According to the research results, the highest ranked strengths of the study participants were:

- **Strategic**: sorts through the clutter and finds the best route; sees patterns where others see complexity

- **Achiever**: constant need for achievement

- **Relator**: likes being around close friends; comfortable with intimacy

- **Learner**: always drawn to the process of learning

- **Activator**: impatient for action—once a decision is made, the activator must act

- **Arranger**: a conductor who enjoys managing many variables; always looking for the right configuration

These strengths were best correlated with the values of *family security, honesty, inner harmony, forgiveness,* and the focus on *a comfortable life.* The results revealed that having a higher purpose, belief, is important in the quest for values-based leadership. We will delve deeper into those comparisons later in the book; for now, let's take a look at and break down the top strengths to gain a deeper understanding of their implications.

A Deeper Look at the Top Strengths

When taking the Strengthsfinder test from Buckingham's book, only the top five strengths are revealed. Buckingham and Clifton state that focusing on an individual's top strengths exponentially increases the individual's throughput, versus focusing on an individual's weaknesses, which may cause a weakness to become better but not necessarily a strength or unique ability.

As mentioned previously, the following strengths contain the highest concentration: Strategic, Achiever, Relator, Learner, Activator, and Arranger. My study results demonstrated the **thinking** talent theme (learning style) as having the highest concentration, followed by the **striving** talent theme (personal motivation).

Strategic Strength

The Strategic strength had the highest ranking in the study. This is no surprise since executive-level leaders need to have the ability to sort through the clutter, find the best route, and see patterns where others see complexity. It is important to note that 50 percent of all interviewed groups (business, finance, and military) had the strength **Strategic**, as this is a necessary strength for senior-level executives. In order for them to run their business, it is important to take a strategic view of their organizations.

A great example of a leader with the Strategic strength is Lt. General Mick Kicklighter of the US Army. He was asked to take on a mission by then Secretary of Defense, Donald Rumsfeld. The mission was to prepare a plan to close down the Coalition Provisional Authority (CPA), and simultaneously assist the Department of State to develop planning to stand a US Embassy and assist in overseeing the implementation of these plans. This had to be accomplished and synchronized with return of sovereignty of the nation to the Iraqi people. This all had to occur at the same time. Though handpicked for the mission, Lt. Gen. Kicklighter both recognized that the task at hand was daunting and appreciated that he would not be able to complete it alone. Once he fully understood the parameters of the mission, he began to think strategically about the people, resources, and time needed to get the job done:

The first thing was to build a core of very competent, very dedicated, very professional people who were very committed to the mission and would move heaven and earth to get it done. The State Department called me over to assist in building a parallel team. I knew all of the senior leaders in the State Department, so that was a great strength, knowing who they were and knowing I could count on them to support this as well. It was a very daunting task to make it all happen, but it was one of those times when you're like a deer caught in the headlights. They ask you to do this tremendous, what you think is almost an overwhelming mission, and yet you can't say no—you've got to go for it.

Lt. Gen. Mick Kicklighter used his Strategic strength to surround himself with the right team in order to complete his mission, which was completed two days earlier than the deadline, catching everyone by surprise, including the media and Al-Qaeda. We can do the same in everyday life as we strategically surround ourselves with people who are competent, dedicated, professional, and committed to the task at hand, whether we are on the job or simply navigating our way through life.

In the study, those leaders with Strategic as their highest strength had surprisingly similar rankings for their talent themes. Lt. Gen. Kicklighter, along with the other respondents who tested as

Strategic, gave higher importance rankings to Comfortable Life, Health, Sense of Accomplishment, and Imaginative.

Evaluating the Rankings

The direct correlation between the Strategic strength and the above values could be so strong because they are broad in nature and require strategic thinking in order to accomplish their goals. The strategic leader looks to find the best possible solution to make it easiest. They work through their people to get the job done. This translates to having a better life where they can take the time to think in the midst of handling many tasks at the same time and being healthy in order to get the job done, which takes imagination and produces a high sense of accomplishment.

These themes also have to do with taking care of oneself and others. Comfortable life correlates to having balance in their life, which is something all high-level leaders struggle with, and characterize as highly important. Health is something that everyone talked about in their interviews; they exercise regularly and eat healthy. Even when they are on the road, they are careful with their diet.

Strategic leaders feel a sense of accomplishment when they make an impact in people's lives and are creative in the way they approach their business and their life. That creativity underscores the idea that Strategic people find alternative solutions as they sort through the chaos to bring order. Interestingly enough, their low ranking on Equality and Loving indicates that they don't need to be treated equally nor do they treat others equally; they employ what I call **The Platinum Rule**: *Do unto others as **they** would like done onto **them**.* They understand that everyone has their own strengths (their genius) and should be treated according to how THEY need to be coached, managed, and trained, not by "using broad strokes" and treating everyone the same. They derive most of their satisfaction in life from their work achievements, hence the low ranking for *Loving*. They are so busy finding the best route that, at times they don't stop to "smell the roses," and miss loving altogether. This is something leaders must watch, remembering that at the end of their life, family is what will matter most to them and lack of time with their family is what people most regret.

QUESTIONS TO KEEP YOU THINKING

1. Which top strengths do you most identify with and how do you use these strengths in your current role as a leader?

   a. **Strategic**: sorts through the clutter and finds the best route; sees patterns where others see complexity

   b. **Achiever**: constant need for achievement

   c. **Relator**: likes being around close friends; comfortable with intimacy

   d. **Learner**: always drawn to the process of learning

   e. **Activator**: impatient for action—once a decision is made, the activator must act

   f. **Arranger**: a conductor who enjoys managing many variables; always looking for the right configuration

2. What is the "double edge sword" of each of your strengths and how does that manifest in your role as a leader?

3. How does balance play a role in your life as a leader? Be specific.

Achiever Strength

The next highest ranking was that of Achiever. No surprise there. Those respondents who had Achiever as one of their strengths gave higher importance rankings to the values of Imaginative and Pleasure and lower importance rankings to Forgiving and Loving. Achievers start every day at zero, have a constant need for achievement, and *need* to achieve something tangible in order to feel good about themselves.

Evaluating the Rankings

The **Achiever** strength was found in 50 percent of business and military leaders, but only in 25 percent of finance leaders. This could be because in the military, when a leader does not achieve his or her goal, this could result in the loss of people's lives. Likewise, entrepreneurial organizations rely on achieving their goals; otherwise the organization's livelihood is at stake.

Achievers obviously have a constant need for achievement. It has already been established that military and business leaders have a different view of achievement of a goal, as in the military, the leaders' decisions constitute saving or losing lives, whereas in entrepreneurial organizations, leaders' decisions constitute the livelihood of the business. When leaders are focused on achieving goals that have high risk, there is little time for close relationships requiring love and forgiveness. Instead of viewing the tough times as opportunities for reconciliation or forgiveness, they view them as lessons learned. Understandably, the Achievers in this study appeared to find great pleasure in achieving their goals and growing their people.

Matt Toledo, CEO and editor of the Los Angeles Business Journal, mentioned how he loves helping people reach their dreams. When asked what he likes about his field, he talked about dream making, helping individuals and companies realize their dreams and helping them get there. Maria Salinas, chairwoman of ProAmerica Bank at the time of this writing, says of developing her people:

> *I'm a big believer in growing people, I really am. I think that it starts with open and honest communication about where you want to be. If it's somewhere else, let's talk about it. I have had people work for me who have left to go get a better job or promotion somewhere else. And I've always viewed that as my success because I helped them get there.*

Ms. Salinas clearly finds a sense of achievement in both meeting her own goals, which she has worked hard to accomplish, and developing the teams around her. It is a win-win for her people as they trust her to guide them to where they long to be in their career.

From the military perspective, achievement is an integral part of military hierarchy and advancement. It's no wonder that 50 percent of the military leaders interviewed had this strength as their highest strength. US Navy command surgeon Vice Admiral Raquel Bono is as tough and no-nonsense as they come, but she loves the interaction with her patients and being part of the solution for their lives. She recalls being sent to a war zone to perform surgery:

Those of us in the medical field get a little full of ourselves. Because we're at the top of the chain, surgeons, feel we are better than others. I realized I am only a very small piece of what's going on in the war. That's when I really began to appreciate being a part of a bigger purpose. So many of us feel we're being asked to do things that we would never do, like doing surgery in the middle of a combat zone; if the goal is to save someone's life, shouldn't I be doing whatever it takes to make it happen? It was a matter of being able to apply the best kind of medicine in a challenging situation.

Bono's higher purpose was saving lives; that is what kept her focused on the task at hand. There are many examples that reinforce Achievers finding pleasure in the achievement. For Rear Admiral Rachel Bono, it was performing surgery in the middle of a combat zone or making sure that her patients were cared for with excellence; for one business leader, it was competing at the Pomona finals with the fastest race car; and for another, it was taking over a company as the CEO and turning it around in six months. The mere achievement of their goal was enough for these leaders.

Notice that Rear Admiral Bono mentioned her appreciation for being part of a bigger purpose. Values-based leaders with Achiever as their highest strength are driven to achieve, and they are also driven to make a difference in the lives of those around them and work with a higher purpose in mind; being part of something bigger than themselves. Finding and working in your purpose is a key part of maximizing your genius.

QUESTIONS TO KEEP YOU THINKING

1. Do you feel you have to accomplish something tangible in order to feel good about yourself each day? If the answer is yes, you may have *Achiever* in your top five strengths.

2. The participants in the study who tested as *Achievers* also gave high ranking to Imaginative and Pleasure and lower ranking to Forgiving and Loving. If you answered yes to question number 1, how does this play out in your professional and personal life?

3. How have you established a sense of achievement in your organization?

4. How do you ensure the performance is sustainable?

Relator Strength

The **Relator** strength had the same frequency as the Achiever strength. The high frequency of this theme pattern may not seem to fit with high-level executives or military leaders, but this theme is the first one that appears to distinguish the values-based leader from the average high-profile leader. Those respondents who had *Relator* as one of their strengths gave higher importance rankings to Forgiving, Inner Harmony, and Broad-Minded. These Relators also gave lower importance rankings to Capable and Self-Controlled.

Evaluating the Rankings

Relators derive a great deal of pleasure from being around close friends and are comfortable with intimacy. This strength surfaced in 50 percent of the business and finance leaders, but in only 25 percent of the military leaders. Why such a low percentage found in military generals? One could argue that military leaders don't need to relate to their soldiers, as the rank dictates that the soldiers must follow the orders of their superiors. In fact, according to an ex-marine, officers and the enlisted personnel are not permitted to commingle away from their duties, as it is called fraternization.

The leaders with Relator in their top five strengths had high rating of the values Forgiving, Inner Harmony, and Broad-Minded, all of which are necessary for top leadership positions.

But how does this strength translate to the business world?

In a 1999 *Fortune Magazine* article titled, "Why CEOs Fail," Ram Charan and Geoffrey Colvin speculate that many CEOs usually know there is a problem in their organization; their "inner voice" is telling them, but they suppress it. The failure is one of emotional strength. The Relator theme pattern would have much to add to emotional strength, and leaders who persevere tend to have that caliber of emotional intelligence.

Relators deliberately encourage deepening relationship and want to understand the goals, fears, and dreams of their colleagues and friends. Chairwoman Maria Salinas shared that she places a high value on getting to know everyone on her team, from the interns all the way up to C-level executives:

> *I take the time to get to know people and what makes them tick. I got some of the greatest ideas from the interns and the financial analysts, the people at the*

very beginning of their leadership journey. I met with everybody, and I thought, you know—there is no substitute for direct communication. It was all very real; I wasn't doing it because I was required to meet with the staff. I've always recommended to my teams to meet with their folks, check in and make sure you understand. It makes for a really great work environment.

This kind of relationship building leads to development of trust. Ms. Salinas' teams still meet for reunions—from her time with the Disney Corporation until now—they were all that close. Trust is huge with Relators, as they desire genuine relationships and are very interested in the character and personality of others. This desire for deep relationships and intimacy correlates directly with emotional intelligence.

In his book on the subject, psychologist Daniel Goleman, PhD, shared the revolutionary idea that emotional intelligence has more to do with success than the traditional view of intelligence or IQ. *The Harvard Business Review* has since hailed emotional intelligence as "a ground-breaking, paradigm-shattering idea," one of the most influential business ideas of the decade. Emotional Intelligence, although not something I tested for in my research, has been correlated with sustainable results. It is the ability to know oneself and to monitor one's own behavior in different circumstances. The ability to relate to others in ways they would like to be related to. Goleman's definition is "the ability to identify, assess, and control one's own emotions, the emotions of others, and that of groups," and this is very similar to the Relator theme.

Executive VP Darrell Brown of US Bank talked about asking the questions: Why? Why not? Why not now? and Why not you? He stated:

> *I put myself in the shoes of those I'm teaching to make sure we are all on the same page and we can gain agreement. The art of asking the right question is how I get confirmation. Inspiration is a matter of the heart for me. People know I hold them accountable, and they like it. I'm a student, constantly reading and learning from others.*

Brown's statement that "inspiration is a matter of the heart" again correlates trust and relationship with overall achievement. Even though he holds people accountable, they like it. Why? Because he has taken the time to ask the right questions in order to learn about and understand his people and what motivates them.

QUESTIONS TO KEEP YOU THINKING

1. How do you view intimacy (deep business relationships) in a business setting?

2. What specifically do you do to make sure your team knows beyond a shadow of a doubt that you care personally about them?

3. How do you inspire your teams today?

Learner Strength

Learners love to learn. They may be often found with a book in their hand or a stack of several on their desk that they are reading simultaneously! Those respondents who had Learner as one of their top strengths gave higher importance rankings to the values Inner Harmony, National Security, A World at Peace, Clean, and Loyal. These Learners also gave lower importance rankings to Family Security, Self-Respect, Honest, and Intellectual.

Evaluating the Rankings

According to Gallup, Learners enjoy the process of learning itself and are energized by the steady and deliberate journey from ignorance to competence. They thrive in dynamic work environments where they are constantly being challenged to learn new subject matter or project details in a short amount of time. This theme spans all three career segments observed in the study—entrepreneurial, finance, and military—as all benefit from the drive to learn quickly.

The Learner strength was found in 50 percent of business and military leaders, and 25 percent of finance leaders. Krames's US Army Leadership Field Manual emphasizes continuous development as a critical part of the culture in the military; leaders are trained from the moment cadets enter training. In the same way, the best leaders are constantly learning; they challenge themselves and consistently look for individuals who can serve as mentors.

Every leader in the study stressed education as fundamental; some made significant sacrifices to get their education, and some were the first in their families to get a college degree. Others expressed regret in either not choosing a high caliber school or not pursuing further post-graduate education, such as a doctorate or MBA. One successful business leader, who received his education long after his business was successful, said about the obstacles he faced in his career:

> *The main obstacle I have encountered was lack of knowledge, experience, and education. Many times I've made mistakes that I would not have made, had I had more knowledge, education, and experience. The lack of education was an obstacle. Someone with an MBA can anticipate things that I wasn't able to anticipate; we have arrived at the same place, but I paid dearly in stress, and have financed mistakes to get the same education.*

The first female general in the US Marine Corps, Major General Angie Salinas (Ret.), mentioned that the military is good about sending its people through preparatory courses to get them ready. There is leadership training from the bottom all the way up to the top, and the learning never ends. Among some of the learning opportunities, the following were mentioned: the Army War College, the National Defense University, Senior Service College. One military leader spent two weeks at Harvard University and one week at the Smith Richardson Foundation. Retired US Army Lt. Gen. Mick Kicklighter, who served for more than thirty-five years as an army officer and fifty years as a public servant, had this to say about being a Learner:

> *Never quit! As a man that will be 77 years old in August, I'm not through learning and not through giving.*

Among this Learning theme, leaders stressed the importance of knowing themselves. One of the business leaders mentioned, "As I become more mature and wiser, I tried to get to know myself very well. My education, for instance, helped me to really dig very, very deep into myself, into the strengths and weaknesses as a human being, and I learned how to be a better leader."

The Learner is always drawn to the process of learning. Learning was mentioned in every face-to-face interview. As mentioned previously, these leaders show high concern for global issues such as national security and world peace; this could be because of their affinity for reading and keeping up with the news. Inner harmony and Clean showed the highest correlation to Learners. The correlation to Inner Harmony could come from the knowledge that they are constantly learning and making themselves better, not allowing themselves to become stale or stagnant.

I was fifteen years old when I had enough credits to graduate from high school. I always did well in school as I really enjoyed the journey of learning new things and sharing them with others. After graduation I remember thinking: "No one asked me about where I will go to college; I guess it's up to me." I started college part time at El Camino College in Torrance and worked full time as the Engineering Department secretary at Deutsch Fasteners Corporation in El Segundo, California, where my mother was employed in the assembly line. I remember thinking: "Someday I will retire my mother." However, I knew I needed to educate myself to get a good position in order to do so. One of the happiest days of my life was the day I called my mother two years after my college graduation, after receiving my first bonus as the youngest branch manager in Southern California at Wells Fargo. I told my mother that day would be her last day she worked in her life, and I asked her to pack her bags as I was taking her on a five-star, first-class trip to Mexico. From that moment on, I have continued to educate myself as a way of making a difference in others. The way I see it today, as leaders, we need to continuously improve ourselves in order to give our very best to others around us; otherwise, we risk becoming stale.

QUESTIONS TO KEEP YOU THINKING

1. In what ways can you identify with the strength of Learner?

2. How do you keep abreast of developments in your field?

3. How do you ensure you are consistently becoming a better leader?

4. How do you share your knowledge with your team and people around you?

5. What actions can you take today to incorporate more learning into your everyday life?

Arranger Strength

The **Arranger** enjoys managing many variables. They are a conductor of sorts, keeping many balls in the air in full control. Arrangers love to find the most productive configuration possible in any given situation.

Among the finance leaders, 50 percent had Arranger in their top five strengths, whereas only 25 percent of the business and military leaders had this strength. Those respondents who had Arranger as one of their top strengths gave higher importance rankings to Honest and True Friend. These Arrangers also gave lower importance rankings to Inner Harmony and National Security, which could simply be a result of their busy nature.

Evaluating the Rankings

The Arranger takes the time to develop true friendship with others, as they have the keen ability to handle many things. The highest correlation with the Arranger was Honesty. When dealing with many issues, it appears necessary to deal with honesty and trust, which are key issues when leading a team. Also, it must be noted that in order to handle many things at the same time, Arrangers have little time to deal with the consequences of dishonesty. They must operate in an honest space, where trust is core—which, according to Steven Covey, increases the speed of performance, as I have seen in my own professional life.

Chairwoman Maria Salinas of ProAmerica Bank already spoke in this chapter to the idea of open communication and really getting to know your people. Open communication is an integral part of the honesty that an Arranger seeks when managing multiple projects and people. From her experience in the corporate world at Disney to her experience as board chairwoman, she pursues open, honest communication as a strategy to manage the many figurative balls in the air:

> *That's really important. The extra piece of communication. Sometimes people need a little more information, so you need to know how to read people and make an effort to follow up with certain individuals in order to make sure they got everything and they're okay. I think as a chair of a board with*

so many dynamic personalities, I have to understand that not everybody is the same. Not everybody processes information the same way. Because I have taken the time to get to know each individual on the board of directors, I have unique insight into who needs a little more information in advance and who needs me to follow up with them after a board meeting. Reacting to those needs is just as important as making those decisions at the table when we meet as a board.

Communication is the resource that fuels an environment of honesty and trust. When asked how she builds trust with her team amidst the many demands of her position, she responded that it comes from spending time with people up front, right from the moment they are hired. She strives to understand the goals and dreams of the individual first so that she can play a vital role in their development as she oversees the overall team: "I just need to know so I can manage their personal and professional goals with them and help them achieve their dreams." For her, losing a team member to a promotion or a better job somewhere else is not failure—it is success. Because she puts the time in from the beginning to understand their needs, she is part of their success long after they leave her sphere of influence. Arrangers, particularly those who are values-based, thrive on managing their people toward success.

QUESTIONS TO KEEP YOU THINKING

1. How do you create an environment of honesty and trust in your organization?

2. When handling multiple projects, how do you make sure all details are handled with every project and critical tasks are handled timely and effectively?

3. What action can you adopt today to keep yourself organized and in control when you are tasked with finding the most productive configurations in your career and in your overall life?

Activator Strength

The **Activator** is always asking, "When can we start?" Though they concede that analysis and debate have their uses, they really want to know when the action is going to begin because that is where their reality begins. Activators will let you know that only action can make things happen. Those respondents who had Activator as one of their top strengths gave higher importance rankings to Independent, Intellectual, Family Security, Pleasure, Self-Respect, and Ambitious. These Activators also gave lower importance rankings to National Security and Responsible.

Among the business and finance leaders, 50 percent had Activator in their top five strengths, while none of the military leaders identified as Activators. The lower percentage of military leaders possessing this strength could be due to the nature of military service where officers follow orders from their superiors and don't "activate" until they are told to do so or when all analysis has been completed.

Evaluating the Rankings

As stated previously, all of the study participants who tested as Activators came from business and finance. That accounts for their independent nature, which is one of the reasons they went into business in the first place. Family security was important to them; in fact, it showed the highest correlation to activators. CEO David Long mentioned his wife is his pillar. She and their children have motivated him to be successful. We will delve more into the support systems of great leaders later in the book.

CEO David Long admits that he can have the tact of a tank when something needs to be done and has high expectations for his team, but he couples that expectation with high rewards. His employees describe him as a coach, mentor, and "cheerleader without the skirt" and understand that he has their best interest at heart.

> *I am passionate about seeing other people succeed. I really like to win, and I need the team in order to do so. I say all the time that we should be better tomorrow than we are today.*

That takes action.

Activators like David Long are ambitious, as evidenced by their mere position. It is interesting to note that National Security and Responsibility are not at the top of the minds of this group. We could infer from the research that Activators are not as concerned with their responsibility as they are with taking action. Values-based leaders with Activator as a main strength know and understand that without action, nothing is accomplished.

QUESTIONS TO KEEP YOU THINKING

1. How does the topic of strength-based leadership affect how you view your own organization?

2. What specific steps can you take to understand your direct report's leadership strengths and the double edge sword of their strengths?

3. Which of the top strengths do you relate to the most? Give examples.

4. How do you keep your values in sync when making critical decisions?

Putting It All Together

According to Gallup, your talents, along with the knowledge and skills gained in life, create your strengths. Just as I learned values-based leadership from my parents and mentors, the participants in my study learned their leadership values from the ones who came before them and walked alongside them in their leadership journey.

In addition, many of the participants came from backgrounds where they had severe financial and relational struggles. Yet one thing they had in common: they all worked through challenges of one kind or another, and this made them stronger.

> WHEN YOU COUPLE STRENGTHS WITH YOUR VALUES DAILY, YOU ARE ABLE TO CREATE SUSTAINABLE RESULTS

U.S. Marine Corps Major General Angie Salinas, with more than thirty-eight years as a leader, was the first in her family to go to college. Initially she did not adjust well to the rigors of academia:

> *After two years of partying and not succeeding in my chosen path, I found myself struggling financially and on my own since my mother moved away. One summer while mailing a letter, a marine recruiter came to me and told me about the opportunity to join the military as a way to create focus in my life. After returning from boot camp, I was inspired by the leaders in the military and how focused they were to make sure their soldiers were successful; I wanted to be just like them.*

She returned to school with a new purpose and made the military her life journey. She attended officer candidate school, kept her grades up, and managed to graduate as *the highest-ranked student in her class*. She had a clear purpose and used her strengths and determination to reach her goal.

In his book, *Authentic Happiness*, psychologist Martin Seligman defines strengths as traits that can be acquired, while talents are innate. Moral strengths such as integrity, honesty, and will (all high on the list of the values-based study participants) are also *values in action*.

Marilyn vos Savant stated that you can never truly eliminate your weaknesses. However, when you know your strengths, you can better utilize them to influence others and help them find their path to success as THEY define it. When you know your strengths and those of your team, you can best leverage those strengths to create the momentum that will ultimately yield desired sustainable results. When you couple strengths with your values daily, you are able to create sustainable results. That's what being a top-level performer and values-based leader is all about!

QUESTIONS TO KEEP YOU THINKING

1. What recurring patterns of thought, behavior, and feeling have made a positive impact on you?

2. In contrast, which negative thoughts, behaviors, and feelings have you allowed to hold you back?

3. What plan can you devise to better utilize your strengths?

4. How does the double-edge sword of your strengths show up in your everyday life?

5. How can you help others understand the double-edge sword of your strengths?

6. Who on your team can you make a difference for today using their strengths to motivate and encourage positive change?

CHAPTER SUMMARY – Key Takeaways

* Values-based leaders had these StrengthsFinder results as their top strengths: Strategic, Achiever, Relator, Learner, Activator, and Arranger.

* Top-level performers are also learners and embrace feedback from their team.

* In order to be a great leader, one must also be a great follower.

- During times of crisis, people reveal their true self – take a front row seat and observe their actions.

- Leading with your strengths and leveraging the strengths of people around you can cause a momentum of positive change that is exponentially greater than trying to make up for weaknesses.

- Understanding the double-edge sword of your strengths and helping others do the same is critical in creating trust with others.

- You can put your values in action through honesty, integrity, and courage in your decision process.

CHAPTER THREE

Where You Came From

*Pivotal moments in our lives shape our values
and determine both our caliber as top-level
leaders and our success.*

Bill George, a leadership professor at Harvard and author of *Discovering your True North,* talks about authentic leadership being grounded in the understanding of our life journey. I asked many leaders to share a pivotal moment as well as the influential people in their careers. A pivotal moment may be a moment that changed the course of your journey. There may be an interaction with that one person who gave you a chance at a job that changed the trajectory of your career, that serendipitous encounter with someone who turned out to be your mentor and champion, or the moment you met the love of your life. For me, one of my pivotal moments came when I walked into that Wells Fargo Bank branch for the first time with no previous banking experience, full of bravado that fateful day, and declared that I would be bank manager within two years. A bold point, I know, but I made it in one-and-a-half years, nonetheless.

Each and every one of the leaders I talked to had pivotal moments that changed them in some way; some shared pivotal moments that changed the trajectory of their career and their lives.

One of my pivotal moments was when I was serving as branch manager at Wells Fargo. A regional manager position opened up that would oversee twenty-six branches in Southern California; this was the lowest performing region for the bank at the time. It was a daunting task and, on top of everything else, I was six months pregnant. I thought to myself, *I can't apply for this. They will never seriously consider me.* Despite my trepidation, I made up my mind to go for it. I purchased a St. John knit outfit at an upscale department store, had it blocked so my pregnant belly would fit, and I used it for the regional manager interview. And guess what? I got the job! I ended up starting the turnaround of that bank region while I was still pregnant and seeing it through from home for the following three months with a newborn. Yes, it was a massive task as the region, made up of twenty-six branches in Southern California, was rated at the bottom of the bank at the time in all key metrics. This assignment tested and stretched me in ways that I'm not sure I can fully articulate, even to this day. However, without the courage to step out of my comfort zone into a position that I knew would challenge me, I would not have had the opportunity to learn and grow. The moment I decided to take the job was a *defining moment* that started me on a path of successful turnarounds that have led me to where I am today. That particular region ended that year as the #1 performing region, making it to that spot after only six months.

Our history and our decisions shape who we are. Sometimes we don't know the full impact of our decisions until much further down the road, while the impact of others is immediate. Executive Vice President Darrell Brown of US Bank shares how a decision based on a friend's suggestion led to a lifetime career:

> *I wasn't sure what I was going to do. I knew I had the gift of speaking and writing, and I even thought about being a minister. I was on my own at age seventeen, in high school and living alone. After high school a friend told me they were hiring bank tellers. My goal had been to go to law school, but I saw my friends going to law school and working long hours. I decided that's not me. At a time in my life when I needed a push in the right direction, I fell in love with banking.*

That one friend who passed along the information about the bank that was hiring changed the trajectory of his life forever. On his own and without guidance, he started on a path that would, with hard work and determination, led him to become a highly respected servant leader and community advocate. In an April 2014 article in the *LA Sentinel*, staff writer Nicole Williams says that he is unlike any bank executive she has ever met. He thrives on nurturing relationships within the community and advocating for diversity inclusion strategies. Darrell Brown shares what he hopes his legacy will be far beyond the here and now:

> *It's all those things we speak to the same thing we are trying to get to—and that's making a difference for our community, planting seeds for those who are younger so we can bear fruit as we get older and feel comfortable knowing that the legacy is going to live long beyond our years.*

And it all started with the pivotal moment of choosing to go work for a bank.

Pivotal Moments Are Opportunities to Learn

Our pivotal moments will not always be positive ones. I know I have dealt with my share of negative experiences in my life, however, I see negative experiences as an opportunity to pursue growth and develop character. Years ago, one of my superiors from a past employer who has since retired told me: "I'm going to shove something down Betty's throat." I learned then that he was going to place someone in a leadership position in another state that I led, and I did not agree with the decision. Though his selection was the wrong person to lead the company in that capacity due to a lack of experience in that field, I decided I would align and make the individual the very best leader under the circumstances. Although I was put off by his behavior and blatant disrespect for me, I made a conscious, non-emotional decision to consider the following:

Is he a bully, or is he simply under a lot of stress?

Did he mean to disrespect me in that fashion?

I did my research, talked to people, and concluded that he was not a bully so there must be another reason for his behavior. The next week at a one-on-one session with that person, I told him how I had considered both the options of bully or stress and shared with him what I had found. I then asked him, "Are you under a lot of stress?" He answered, "Actually, Betty, yes I am." I thanked him for his honesty and told him, "You need to know something about me. My father taught me to be a woman of honor. I have your back.

I've never been disrespectful in any way toward you. I expect the same respect from you." From that moment on, he was my greatest advocate. He even wrote a stellar letter of recommendation for my entry into Pepperdine's doctoral program.

The lesson here?

As leaders, we can't afford to make assumptions about the people with whom we interact and work. We have to do our research and find out the root causes of people's behavior without making assumptions based on our own personal experience. The information I discovered led to a stronger, more respectful relationship with him because I chose to understand the person behind the behavior. By giving this person the benefit of the doubt, I was able to build trust with one of the key leaders in the company and, as a result, he became my greatest fan inside and outside the organization.

In life you will experience pivotal moments where you are faced with a decision to engage in a positive way or a negative way. It's up to you how you choose to behave.

How many times have you judged someone, only to find out you were wrong?

Even when we strive to live and lead with values, we will undoubtedly make mistakes in our journey. In the same way that we can choose how to handle negative experiences, we can decide to use our mistakes as opportunities to learn. That is what top-level leaders do every single day. CEO Alex Fortunati shares a decision made as a young person that had both immediate negative consequences and long-term positive ones:

When I was very young, around sixteen or seventeen, I was working for a transportation company in Argentina. I was very lucky to be there. At the time, I had already been working for a few years and was offered the transportation company job because I knew languages: Spanish, English, and Italian. So someone referred me to this German subsidiary that had offices in Buenos Aires and they said, "You know, with your knowledge of languages, you would be great working for the air cargo department," so I went on to work with them. I was young, but I always had a smile on my face and behaved like a gentleman.

What I didn't realize until about a year into the position was that I would be at the wrong place at the wrong time.

One day, one my bosses took me and a few other coworkers to a cargo case and offered some of the cargo (ties) to us for free. I felt it was wrong, and refused initially, but the boss said, "Take this," and I finally relented. I was young and should have had the courage to resist. Word of the incident made its way up to the managing director, and the three other men involved were fired. The managing director asked if I was going to resign, and I humbly responded that it was an accident, I was so sorry, and I understood his decision.

I didn't yet have thoughts of becoming an entrepreneur or having my own company. I was just a shy, nice kid who had traveled around the world because of my family. After the incident, I asked a customs broker friend if he would give me the opportunity to work for him. "Whatever services you want for your cargo, I will put the knowledge that I learned in the last year—document preparation and all that—to work for you. If you just let me use a desk and a phone, I will do it for free."

In my role, I was forced to go out on cold calls, knock on doors. I was still very fortunate to get some appointments from that and gain customers, but the most valuable part of that experience was what I was learning in the trenches, so to speak. I was learning how to articulate, how to present, how to dress better, and how to guide conversations.

Years later, Alex still practices those very basic tenets of presenting oneself in a positive, polished way, which has given him a solid foundation to build upon his thirty years of successful business leadership experience. Values are always at the forefront of his mind as he leads. He may have been "at the wrong place at the wrong time" at that distribution center in Argentina long ago, but he certainly learned many of the *right* ways to do business as a result. Alex has been featured in both *Hispanic Executive* and *American Executive* magazines and was named Entrepreneur of the Year by the former. He is known for building his facilities-maintenance powerhouse company from the ground up and helping customers do what makes them successful every day.

Clearly, he has done a lot of things right.

Pivotal Moments Help Us Discover Who We Are

Some of our pivotal moments are self-propelled and others are more fortuitous, yet they all shape us. My hope is that you see yourself in some of the pivotal moments that I share in these pages. CEO of *Latina Style* Magazine Robert Bard had a pivotal moment in the mid-70s while working at the LA Times. It was a connection that brought him back to his heritage:

> *At that time I had no Hispanic influence in my life—my world was the mainstream world. Since I came from Chile, I went to school as a foreign student, a very prestigious school for foreign dignitaries and members of the French delegation in Chile. I grew up in an environment that was very privileged. I had the opportunity to meet with Maury Rosas, the highest Latino executive at Pacific Bell. We really hit it off, and he introduced me to my Hispanic Heritage. Nothing I grew up with compared with the experience of the Hispanic community, and I found myself being persistently recruited by my new friend to join the MALDEF (Mexican American Legal Defense and Educational Fund) leadership program. Maury was the chair of the program and put me in the class. Completely unprepared, I showed up for the classes to learn something. I went through the MALDEF leadership program, and that is what connected me to the Hispanic community.*

As part of my MALDEF leadership training program, I was asked to select a Hispanic mentor. I've never been shy, so I looked for the highest Hispanic official, Jerry Apodaca, the governor of New Mexico. I called and introduced myself & explained my training program, and he understood, being on the board of MALDEF as well. I explained that I would only need a few minutes of his time and left it at that. At three in the morning, the phone rings, waking me up, and it's the governor. Quickly trying to shake off sleep, I explained why I had chosen him as a potential mentor rather than someone in LA. "If I'm really going to engage," I explained, "I want the big picture, not just a microcosm of this community." There was a pregnant pause and he said, "These are the rules. Anything I tell you to do, don't question me. This is like military mentorship; you will have to follow my directions." At the time, I had no idea how much that would change my life.

From that one pivotal decision, his life took on a new trajectory, as he was connected to the people who would be pivotal to his current role as CEO of Latina Style Magazine, the most influential publication reaching the contemporary Hispanic woman with readership over 600,000. Undaunted by the scope of what he was reaching for initially, he took a risk and was rewarded with a mentoring relationship that bolstered his career. He had forgotten where he came from, and fully embracing and remembering his roots brought him both fulfillment and success.

QUESTIONS TO KEEP YOU THINKING

1. Can you point to any experiences you had as a young person that have positively influenced who you are today? Explain.

2. What about negative experiences? Have they influenced you in a positive or negative way? Explain.

3. Can you point out an experience (positive or negative) that positively impacted the key people in your leadership team?

4. Have you experienced the benefits of having a mentor guide you to new heights, and a greater vision for who you are, as Robert Bard experienced?

5. Describe a pivotal moment in your life and explain how it affected your personal, career, or life journey.

Pivotal Moments Help Clarify Our Vision

Even when we are set on a path in our lives or career, our experiences can serve as tools to clarify our vision and purpose. If we are always living according to our values, even the most seemingly insignificant interactions can lead to unexpected success.

> YOU NEVER KNOW WHO PEOPLE ARE OR HOW THEY WILL TAKE YOUR MESSAGE —ALWAYS, ALWAYS, ALWAYS TREAT PEOPLE WITH LOVE, RESPECT, AND DIGNITY, PUTTING YOURSELF IN THEIR SHOES. YOU WILL NEVER REGRET LIVING WITH THAT VALUE.

Early in my career when I worked as a loan officer at a major bank in California, I would often stay late working at the office. I worked so late, in fact, that I ended up befriending the cleaning people who came long after the doors closed each night. I had been at this particular bank six months, and I was determined to exceed my goals. (At that time, I was given the goal of bringing into the bank a certain number of new relationships, which consisted of checking accounts, savings accounts and loans.) One evening while I was working late once again, the cleaning crew—consisting of a husband, wife, and their children—came to do their usual work. I could tell the husband was waiting for me to finish my work in order to talk to me.

He finally came over, quietly mentioned he wanted to consider some investments, and asked what programs would be right for him. I answered that it just depended on how much he wanted to invest. My jaw dropped when he said, "I have $30,000." Wow. When I asked him how he had accumulated so much money, he explained that he and his wife had been saving money since they came from Central America. I ended up finding him the perfect investment program for his needs, and I also learned a valuable lesson.

How many times in our life do we judge people by their occupation, the way they look, the car they drive, or their way of being? My mother always told me: "We are similar to others and no one is better than we are; they may have more debt, but we are all the same children of God, and we must treat others as such." If I had not treated his family with love, respect, and dignity, I would have missed out on the opportunity to create a successful situation for everyone involved. The Golden Rule is something I grew up with in North America: "Treat others like you would like to be treated." I came up with **The Platinum Rule**: *"Treat others like THEY would like to be treated."* You never know who people are or how they will take your message —always, always, always treat people with love, respect, and dignity, putting yourself in their shoes. You will never regret living with that value.

I have been honored to have gotten to know many high-level military leaders during the interviewing process of my study; many of them are now trusted friends. One of these exceptional leaders is Vice Admiral Raquel C. Bono, US Navy command surgeon, who at the time of her interview had thirty-three years' experience as a navy officer. Today she leads from Washington, D.C. and is in charge of health care for the Armed Forces in the United States. A big job!!! She leads her people with a deep desire to make a positive impact in every situation she commands. With a background in the US Navy, Admiral Bono subscribes to the following command philosophy:

> **A** - Always ready to answer the call: our people trained and prepared, physically, and mentally; our craft and equipment properly maintained.
>
> **C** - Competence in our trade, seamanship and defensive combat skills.
>
> **B** - Bring out the best in our sailors: as a unit, teams, and individuals.
>
> **O** - One team: one fight, with every sailor respected, every sailor accountable.

N - Never compromise on safety; make it your first consideration and your second nature.

E - Excellence in all we do: reflect pride in who you are and what you represent.

EVERYONE BENEFITS WHEN A LEADER, REGARDLESS OF MILITARY OR CIVILIAN AFFILIATION, LEADS WITH EXCELLENCE OF VISION, STRATEGY, AND PHILOSOPHY.

When she was deployed during the first gulf war in 1989, Bono was put in charge of casualties. She was only there for seven months, and encountered several critical injuries during that time. She found that she was pretty good at being a department head and could combine helping to maintain the rules and ensuring the staff, nurses, and foremen were effective in making them come together to deliver the best care for their patients. In her career, she always sought to understand where her colleagues were coming from as well as championing her many patients. It was during this time, however, that she had an epiphany of sorts:

> *So many of us feel we're being asked to do things we would never do (surgery in the middle of a combat zone), but if the goal is to save someone, shouldn't I be doing whatever it takes to make it happen? So, yes, I'm a surgeon, but I'm also serving the bigger purpose of saving lives and doing it with excellence, whatever it takes.*

As she realized her greater purpose and focused her vision in that pivotal moment, Bono was able to make a greater positive impact in her field of navy command surgery. Her patients were better represented and championed, and her colleagues were better heard and managed. Everyone benefits when a leader, regardless of military or civilian affiliation, leads with excellence of vision, strategy, and philosophy.

As values-centered leaders, it is up to us to realize what our "bigger purpose" is in our career, field, or chosen life path. It doesn't have to be as dramatic as literally saving someone's life, but it could have the same impact if done with perseverance and excellence.

If you are a head of state or a C-level executive at the top of your game, take the time to be a mentor for someone. If you are an up-and-coming leader or simply looking for guidance from someone who has been where you are now, seek out someone to mentor you; you can also reverse-mentor them in return. Wherever you are in your career or in your life, know that it doesn't have to be your stopping point. Be passionate about what you're doing and at the same time, be a part of someone else's pivotal moments by looking to make a positive impact in others.

> IN THOSE PIVOTAL **CRUCIBLE** MOMENTS, THOSE WHO LEAD WITH VALUES WILL CHOOSE THE PATH THAT HONORS THEIR CHARACTER & INTEGRITY, WHICH THEN LEADS TO POSITIVE CHANGE.

As you navigate the challenges of your day-to-day life, look at each and every experience you have, whether positive or negative, as a potential classroom for your personal development. If you're not happy where you are, change your situation. As Greg Jacobson says in his bestselling book, "Our culture in the US is driven by ambition and aspiration, and always looking for the next level—but if ambition and aspiration stops us from being happy with what we have now, then we're missing what it's all about." What's the use of being successful if we can't be happy? So many people pursue being successful, and they confuse being successful with being happy. The participants in my study prove that you are never done learning and growing. You can be happy even as you navigate setbacks, and successes are an opportunity for learning. Both contribute to overall growth.

Lead with values first and you will never go wrong.

QUESTIONS TO KEEP YOU THINKING

1. Do you have a working vision or strategy in your life? How about in your career? Can you articulate it in no more than one sentence?

2. When was the last time you made a tough decision leading with your "higher purpose?"

3. How can you influence others around you to do the same?

4. If you have not found your "higher purpose" like Vice Admiral Raquel Bono did during the first gulf war, what action can you take today to discover it?

CHAPTER SUMMARY – Key Takeaways

× Be mindful of pivotal moments, whether personal or career related. Always remember: breakdowns are specifically designed to create breakthroughs…if you work through them.

* Look for your "higher purpose" in the everyday realities of your career.

* Values-based leaders can emerge from any career, sector or walk of life.

* Some of the most successful people found their careers by accident. Just follow your passion and the rest will come.

* Both positive and negative experiences can influence your life journey; be sure that they are having a positive overall influence.

* Your life and career will undoubtedly contain pivotal moments. You simply have to recognize them, positive or negative, for what they are—a means for development.

* Be clear about your vision and discover your deeper purpose in everything you do. Remember: Values-based leaders' actions line up with their values. Integrity is mission-critical, as is focusing on the good of the whole, and making a positive impact in others.

* In those pivotal *crucible* moments, those who lead with values will choose the path that honors their character & integrity, which then leads to positive change.

CHAPTER FOUR

Motivation to Lead

Leading and Living With a Higher Purpose

What gets you out of bed in the morning?

It could be a sense of obligation, the dinging of your smartphone with an early barrage of emails to attend to, or the promise of a paycheck or big payoff. For the leaders I interviewed, the motivation to lead was so much more. It included creating value for others, impacting change, mentoring others, personal achievement, purpose in life, and taking care of others. Almost every executive I interviewed in my study shared that they lived and led others with a higher purpose in mind.

What is my motivation to lead?

For me, it is about creating a legacy that will last long after I am gone from this earth. It is to make a positive impact in the world by creating a social epidemic of injecting values back into leadership, to have a positive impact in the world, one person at a time.

My mother passed away when I was in my twenties. She was my best friend, someone whom I could call in times of heartache and celebration. When my father passed away, all of a sudden I was nobody's daughter. I suddenly felt like it was up to me. *I felt the need to leave a legacy for my children.* My mother took care of the people who cleaned the streets, fed people at the church, and extended help to anyone who needed it. She would invite them in and serve them dinner, gathering up our toys and clothes to send home with them. She had a big heart that knew no boundary. My father helped his eleven brothers and sisters, and anyone who was in need could rely on my father to lend them a hand.

I am my parent's daughter, and I too want to take care of those less fortunate. When I graduated with my doctorate, I received honors for my dissertation and had zero debt. Throughout my life and my career, I have discovered that true success comes from building trust and adding value in relationship for generations. I had nothing when I came to the United States. As I mentioned in the dedication of this book, my brother Fernando gave me my first $500 scholarship and encouraged me to get an education. Now I have a deep desire to pay it forward. My vision has grown to extend far beyond the boundaries of my immediate spheres of influence. I have come to understand that I am a citizen of the world and that there is a commonality between all of the cultures. We are all God's children. It doesn't really matter where you came from—my legacy is for all mankind.

My overarching goal is to provide for 100 underserved children in each of the seven continents before I turn 80 years old. That is 700 scholarships around the world. The criteria for my scholarships are as follows:

1. They must be values-based servant leaders, students who are already helping others in their journey.

2. They must want to study business or science, where their career will be used for the good of society and being examples for others.

3. They must agree to pay it forward by giving away a minimum of one scholarship with similar criteria. This will be the beginning of a sustainable legacy.

Soon after I returned from Kenya, where I visited with a number of values-based high school students, I decided to team up with Cynthia Kersey and the Los Angeles-based Unstoppable Foundation, a non-profit humanitarian organization that brings sustainable education to children and communities in developing countries. Through this organization, I hope to provide 100 scholarships in Africa. I have also teamed up with Bob Carr's *Give Something Back Foundation* where underserved students in North America are supported with full college scholarships. This is another noteworthy organization led by someone I trust.

I have decided to donate 50 percent of the proceeds of this book to create seed money for my dream. By the time I reach the age of eighty, I will have given out 100 scholarships in each continent—yes, 700 full college scholarships—to young values-based, high-performing servant leaders who have already demonstrated the art of paying it forward. If you do the math, this movement has the possibility of creating an epidemic of paying education forward around the world.

Now do you agree we could make a positive impact in the world, one person at a time?

I do. One person at a time.

My vision is to ignite Heads of State, CEOs, C-level executives, and up-and-coming high potential leaders, with the spark of values-centered leadership in their spheres of influence in order to make a positive impact in the world.

I want to ignite that spark in *you* as well.

What is your motivation to lead—what gets you out of bed in the morning? To lead with values, you must find more than just a sense of obligation to motivate you to lead others well. You must find your *why*. I am reminded of Sheryl Sandberg's definition of leadership:

> *Leadership is about making others better as a result of your presence and making sure that impact lasts in your absence.*

I have strived to achieve this in every individual I have been entrusted to lead. I also heard that sentiment resonate time and again while interviewing the amazing men and women I studied. Each and every one of these high-level executives and military leaders expressed a deep sense of desire for deeper purpose.

Their motivation to lead included:

These motivations suggest a servant-leader attitude, revealed during the interviews. The leaders showcased in this book all gave high rankings to those values which reflected their personal integrity and desire to *lead with a higher purpose*. They all mentioned mentors who inspired them, were good listeners, allowing others' honest, courageous feedback and direction.

In my study, each of these values is correlated to the top leadership strengths in the table below.

Correlation of Highest Concentration of Top Strengths to Motivation to Lead

Top Strength	Motivation to Lead
Strategic	Impacting change, creating value, purpose in life
Achiever	Impacting change, creating value, personal achievement
Relator	Taking care of people, mentoring others, patriotism
Learner	Personal achievement
Arranger	Creating value, impacting change, philanthropic
Activator	Driven, self-discipline, responsible

Motivation: Creating Value for Others

As evidenced by the chart above, the top strengths exhibited by the participants had direct correlation to their motivation to lead. There was an obvious connection to creating value for others as one of the motivations to lead for those with Strategic, Achiever and Arranger in their top five strengths.

Matt Toledo, CEO of the *Los Angeles Business Journal*, answered my question of, "Tell me about what motivates you to lead—what drives you?" Without hesitation he replied, "Creating Value for others."

"Creating value for others," he replied.

When I asked, "What do you mean by value?" he replied:

> *I mean creating value for others and creating greater value for my business at the same time. I think good leaders get results working with and through people. I have a desire, really a mission, to help people figure out what they want, and to help them get it. It's tremendously motivating for people when you take an interest in them and what they want—they get excited, want to do well, want to succeed, and want to work hard for you.*

When I asked, "How do you find out what people want?" he answered:

> *You find out what they want through investing time with them, asking them questions, helping them to eliminate the noise in their minds. When you get to this level of relationship and the essence of who they are, you learn what they are really passionate about. But it takes time to wade through all the noise and find that central idea that inspires them. Once you discover that, people light up! They totally light up!*

Matt Toledo gets it. When you create value for others and take the time to invest in them, discovering their wants, it ignites a passion and excitement in them that makes them *want* to do well and work harder for you as their leader. It's the law of reciprocity in practice.

Of course, in order to go this deep with your people, you must first create trust with them. Have you experienced leaders acting like a bull in a china shop, changing the organization without first creating an environment of trust? I have seen leaders who have created short-term wins, sacrificing sustainable performance just to please their superiors, make a good impression, or put money in their pockets. I have found that some of these quick wins, however, are short lived and absent of trust creation. The only way to build sustainable results is by first creating trust with your people and then, and only then, applying change, which they can live with now because they will trust you. The leader can then create greater sustainability in the change by embedding the change as part of the new culture.

Retired Lt. General Mick Kicklighter speaks about trust as a critical factor with those he recruits. Because of that, integrity of character is always high on his list. This distinction makes sense, especially in a military setting, where they all must trust people with your life. "The General," as other high-ranking military leaders fondly call him, is a man of honor, character and truth. This is critical in the military setting, where one must trust one-another, with their lives. In his book *The Speed of Trust*, Steven Covey, Jr. speaks about the phenomenon of building trust quickly in an organization. He asserts that *trust creation is the center point of sustainable, high performance in an organization.*

When I joined California Bank & Trust, my first focus was building trust with the people in the organization. In the first three months, I had face-to-face conversations with over 550 people, asking them to answer just three questions: 1) what's working, 2) what's not working, and 3) If you had a magic wand, what would you do differently? My "magic wand" became very popular quickly. As I traveled around the state, I looked for opportunities to WOW my people in a way that personally touched them: replacing an old couch in the lunch room, a new refrigerator, air conditioner repaired right away, a phone call to the head of a department fixing an issue on the spot, a hug, a story about my students or my personal journey. These face-to-face meetings generated a crescendo of trust creation that yielded dividends along the way. When people realized that I was real, that I genuinely cared about them (and I showed it with my actions), that is when the transformation began…but not until they trusted me.

CEO of MyEmployees David Long models building trust in a unique way with his organizational book clubs. He creates value for his employees by purchasing books and freeing up time each week to allow them to discuss the content. These aren't just books about how to be a better employee, however—these are books about relationships, managing personal finances, and attaining and sustaining a better quality of life. Why would he go through all that trouble? Because he understands that creating value for his people by improving their lives has a reciprocal effect on their work lives. Any time or money "lost" on book clubs in the short term is more than made up for in positive attitude, buy-in, and productivity in the long run. And he truly loves to see his people succeed in both their personal and professional lives.

> WHEN PEOPLE REALIZED THAT I WAS FOR REAL, THAT I GENUINELY CARED ABOUT THEM (AND I SHOWED IT WITH MY ACTIONS), THAT IS WHEN THE TRANSFORMATION BEGAN…BUT NOT UNTIL THEY TRUSTED ME.

I do something similar at my monthly staff meetings. In our first twelve months together, we reviewed twelve leadership books. All my senior staff meetings begin with a two-hour discussion of a specific book chosen for a specific purpose in our leadership journey together as a team. As a result, the team has grown tremendously. For a list of recommended books, see the Resources page at the back of this book.

I saw how creating value inspires motivation to leaders across the board, from business to military to finance. Creating value for others is a surefire way to encourage both your achievement and the success of everyone around you.

Impacting Change

Impacting change was a prominent motivation to lead amongst the subjects of my study. CEO Alex Fortunati said during his interview that though he is demanding, it is because he wants his people to understand that life is never easy and should never be taken for granted. People need to build their skills, be stronger, and plan in order to be prepared for what life throws at them. That's part of what motivates him to lead people—the sense that he is impacting change in their lives for the better.

> When I see something that needs to be done, I can think of ways to make those things better, whether it is creating programs to address them or whatever it takes. I know I can make an impact because people trust me enough to give me the opportunity to make things happen.

Notice the critical role trust plays in impacting change. Fortunati's people trust him, therefore they will follow his lead. When your team trusts you because you have built that relationship with them through investing in what motivates and inspires them, you can do anything. Like Matt Toledo said, you can then work with people and through them to impact real change in your organization. Impacting change through effective leadership is not limited to the business world, however; you can also use these same principles in your community, social circles and family to make a significant difference.

CEO Matt Toledo's great aunt Lucia was an extraordinary leader and entrepreneur thirty-five to forty years ago—quite unique for a Hispanic female back then. She taught him many lessons of tough love, respect and care, and modeled how to impact the lives of others:

> *I would go to her shop and I watched her take care of customers. I watched her communicate with her workers, people that made patterns and sewed, and I watched her respect everybody; she treated everybody with kindness. As we walked down the street, and as normal in Mexico City, there were beggars on the sidewalks and we walked by one who was sitting down in a doorway and she opened her purse and pulled out a coin purse and grabbed some money and she put it in a woman's hand and she said something just to wish her well and we kept walking; further down the street we encountered another woman standing in a doorway asking for money and I was shocked*

that my aunt had some very harsh words with her and she basically told her she's a strong woman who shouldn't be there begging, and should be working. She said she didn't have any money for her. So these were the lessons of respect, of accountability, of charity, and of holding people responsible and allowing yourself to use your judgment to determine who needed a handout and who needed a little bit of a kick in the bottom to motivate them to be their very best.

Aunt Lucia understood the importance or influencing others for good, whether that was through charity or a "kick in the pants," as she said. Every day we encounter people whom we have the ability to influence from our unique position. It is vital that we are clear on our values so that we can lead and influence from a place of integrity, impacting others along the way.

QUESTIONS TO KEEP YOU THINKING

1. In what tangible ways do you build trust with your employees, friends, and family?

2. Why is it important to find out what people want from their work or personal relationship with you? Explain.

3. Share one way that you can create value for others within your sphere of influence. Get creative!

4. Where in your life or career do you see a need for change? What can you do today to encourage positive changes?

Mentoring Others

I asked everyone in this book about who they were currently mentoring, and every single individual named people they were investing in through a mentoring relationship.

Mentorship can play a pivotal role in your development as a leader, and it is profoundly important in your personal development. One of the things I always say when speaking to groups is that when you "make it," and are finally successful, you must go back and take others with you. In the earlier quote by Sheryl Sandberg, we observe that *leadership is about making others better as a result of your presence and making a lasting impact*—that is what mentoring is all about. When someone mentors you, they help you see the potential you do not see in yourself, and guide you to dream bigger and better and even to implement those dreams.

CEO Shaheen Sadeghi, founder of LAB Enterprise and former president of Quicksilver, mentors twelve to fifteen people a year. Pablo Schneider is never without an intern at any event or conference he attends. It is not unusual to get an email from Pablo introducing a potential mentee, or Pablo showing up to an event with multiple mentees to learn from the experience and get introduced to potential employers or mentors.

One of the other study participants who holds an executive position in banking shared how his mentor Margie LaForce made an amazing impact on his life:

> *She made me feel smarter and better than I felt about myself. She gave me hope! She treated me and talked to me as if I were this young Einstein and I could do*

anything I wanted, even though I was dirt poor after failing. She created a confidence in me that nobody else did!

IT DOESN'T TAKE A LOT OF TIME, JUST QUALITY TIME WITHOUT TELEVISION OR SOCIAL MEDIA STANDING IN THE WAY OF TRUE DIALOGUE FROM ONE HUMAN BEING TO ANOTHER.

He went on to explain how having mentors allowed him to develop the confidence to think analytically about everything he did, even influencing his management style (more on that later). He came to understand that it was important to understand people's wants and needs and work **with** people rather than **over** them. His mentor influenced him in such a way that he turned around and as a result he now motivates and challenges thousands of others.

I can relate to this story. As I was growing up, my mother used to tell me that I was super intelligent and could do anything I set my mind to if I worked hard enough and believed in myself. She truly believed in me. I often think about those moments and wonder what my career trajectory would have been like if she hadn't encouraged me like she did during my formative years. It goes to show that the role parents play in their children's education is a critical one. It doesn't take a lot of time, just quality time without television or social media standing in the way of true dialogue from one human being to another.

One way that I have incorporated mentoring into my parenting is through intentionally spending time with each child, pouring my heart and life experiences into them. With that in mind, I took my son Kristopher to India to broaden his sense of the world and expose him to the realities of life beyond North America, both the beautiful and the desolate. We toured the Taj Mahal and were struck by the grandeur of the ivory-white marble mausoleum on the south bank of the Yamuna river, taken in by its history and significance. However, on the way to this magnificent landmark we traveled through streets decimated by poverty. I remember Kristopher saying, "Mama, I want to get out of here." I quickly responded with, "When you look around at the people and conditions here, I want you to realize how blessed you are in North America." It was an important lesson to pass on to my son, and it's one that we all need to remember. I often say: "Children are the messengers we send to a time we will never see."

Mentoring is such a vital part of being a values-based leader because it is how you pass your values on to others and pay it forward to the next generation. Mentors fill the gap between head knowledge and execution. There is nothing better than having someone tell you how valuable you are and that you really can achieve your dreams. In the same way, nothing compares to telling someone they can do it, seeing their eyes light up with belief and self-confidence, and seeing them through to the final accomplishment of their goals. Mentorship is all about making others better as a result of your presence and leaving a lasting impact.

The leaders I interviewed for this book are both mentors AND mentees. Some of us have even chosen reverse mentors who provide feedback for us from several levels below our level. This keeps us grounded.

Personal Achievement

It almost goes without saying that a CEO, military general, or high-level finance executive would be driven by personal achievement, but don't we all strive for that? As leaders, the mark of our effective leadership often hinges on the bottom line of what we have achieved. Henry David Thoreau speaks to this idea quite profoundly:

> *What you **get** by achieving your goals is not as important as what you **become** by achieving your goals.*

Personal achievement showed as a motivation to lead in the Learner and Achiever strengths… of course! In the case of the leaders I interviewed, what they became as a result of their personal achievement speaks for itself. In essence, personal responsibility leads to personal achievement. I can relate to this all too well since I lost my parents so early on in my life. I immediately felt the responsibility that it was up to me to work hard, achieve what I set out to do, love well, and leave a lasting legacy.

CEO Alex Fortunati also dealt with loss, yet at a much younger age. I was so moved with his incredible story of creating the impossible from nothing in his life and career. It is the epitome of a grand personal achievement:

> *As you become more mature and wiser, you try to get to know yourself very well, and Pepperdine did help me in that respect, digging very deeply into my strengths and weaknesses as a human being and how to lead better. But there was one particular incident that really*

*propelled me to achieve what I have achieved in my life—it was my mother and father leaving me and my siblings alone for a year in an apartment in Rome. I was between ten and eleven years old and I had three younger sisters: fourteen, fifteen, and five years old. My parents said they were going to be gone for a few months, but unfortunately it took them a year to come back. I didn't go to school that year. I had to literally **beg** for food.*

Though I was young and loved my parents, I knew that was a mistake. I swore to myself that I was going to do much better in life; I was going to be financially independent; I was going to be a millionaire by age thirty. This obsession to take care of my family began to grow and it motivated me through all the ups and downs. That obsession that my family would never suffer again drove me to keep going, motivated me, and gave me the fuel I needed to want to achieve. It was the obsession to achieve.

Obviously, Fortunati had a strong internal drive to achieve in order to avoid the destitute circumstances he experienced as a young child. You may be driven to achieve by other factors: a family that relies on you financially, parents that expect a level of greatness from you, or employees that depend on the success of your organization in order to be successful themselves. Whether or not you are as driven to achieve as the leaders in my study, you can still learn to navigate your achievements with a greater purpose in mind.

Purpose in Life

Having a "higher purpose" showed up in all the subjects in my study and everyone I have highlighted in this book. It is no surprise, then, that General Mick Kicklighter of the US Army, a master of strategic thinking, speaks to how his career in the armed forces satisfied that deep desire for a purposeful life, and how it involves faith:

> Let me just say that I believe the profession of arms is a very honorable profession, and I gave my life to it. As I come to the end of my life, I would do it again. After I've looked at the world, I would not hesitate. It's not for everybody. I think it's kind of like choosing to be a priest or a nun or a reverend. It requires you to be prepared on any given day to make the ultimate sacrifice for your country, and you've got to understand that.

Many participants talked about a higher being, a personal belief system; some even mentioned having a deep faith in a spiritual being as the center of their life. General Kicklighter added:

> I never saw any conflict between my faith and my duties as a soldier. In fact, when I was in the Middle East, I could be found on a Sunday afternoon at a mosque, a synagogue, a church, and a temple. When asked why, I said, "Because that is where my troops were, and they needed me there, with them at church; not leading from afar, but right there where they were."

General Kicklighter's higher purpose led him to becoming a servant leader to those who served under him. He felt a deep responsibility to lead them right where they were. Now those are values-based leaders whose actions are congruent with their espoused values, focusing on the good of the whole, and making a positive impact on others. When you lead and live with purpose, you are better able to overcome the small things that can often entangle and derail you.

In his book *The Power of Intention*, Dr. Wayne Dyer notes that a sense of purpose is at the very top of the pyramid of self-actualization that American psychologist Dr. Abraham Maslow created over fifty years ago. In his words, "those who feel purposeful are living the highest qualities that humanity has to offer."[9] Dr. Dyer goes on to say that people feel the most purposeful when they are giving their lives away by serving others. In other words, we are the most self-actualized, intentional, and happy when we lead with the higher purpose of giving of ourselves to benefit others.

> WHEN YOU LEAD AND LIVE WITH PURPOSE, YOU ARE BETTER ABLE TO OVERCOME THE SMALL THINGS THAT CAN OFTEN ENTANGLE AND DERAIL YOU.

Taking Care of Others

The concept of taking care of people was woven throughout many of the interviews.

General Mick Kicklighter speaks to the idea that in the army, leadership is responsible to take care of not only the soldiers but also their families:

> *The military is a family and the spouses and children are absolutely important to the mission. The soldiers have to believe and know that their families have a support system that will take care of them. Your job as a leader is to build that system and make sure they know how to reach out, where to go, particularly when there's separation. I felt that the soldiers and their families were one unit and they all sacrifice and give an awful lot.*
>
> *That family unit extends to the battlefield where the soldiers know **why** they are fighting. They know they can depend on you and on each other—that person next to you or behind you or on the other side—because they don't want to let you down just like you don't want to let them down. They're counting on you. I still like the US Army slogan of "be all you can be" because it perfectly represents what we try to do for every soldier who enlists—help and encourage them to be all they can be.*

Dr. Andrew Benton, president and CEO of Pepperdine University for over fifteen years, is a servant leader of the highest caliber and is highly motivated by taking care of others. Though he holds a position of great honor at the university, he and his wife Debby open their home every Sunday to over fifty students:

It's an important act of service, I think, to have them in our home—home is one of my favorite words in the English language—and to feed them a meal that was prepared in our kitchen. It is not catered, as some might expect. Debby and I prepare everything. We often do campouts where the students will bring tents and sleeping bags, I'll move the fire pit to a safe place, and they'll be able to make s'mores and swim in our pool, and use the Jacuzzi, and it's lights out at eleven. I'll make them breakfast the next morning. Why do I do that? It's about connection and relationship.

Dr. Benton makes a point to stop into the cafeteria at lunchtime to make himself available for the occasional student to pass by and ask to sit with him.

I'll just engage them to see if they've got something on their heart that hurts that they want to share or if they're just curious about my journey to this point. I'm always curious about their journey. I make a connection so that when I give them their diploma on the graduation stage, one or four years hence, I've got a connection. It's more than just a handshake or passing connection; it's "I know you." I know about you. I know a bit about what you hope to do. That makes for a much more special moment, I think.

I was meeting Dr. Benton at the university campus to conduct the interview for this book; while there I sent a text to my daughter to see if she had time for a quick meal—she was a Pepperdine student at the time. When I asked Alexandria to meet me at Dr. Benton's office, she said, "I know where his home is, but not his office." That personal touch is such a wonderful trait that sets values-based leaders apart; it's a common thread found amongst the leaders highlighted in this book.

QUESTIONS TO KEEP YOU THINKING

1. What gets you out of bed every morning? Explain.

2. What is your motivation to lead, and why?

3. Can you identify a deeper purpose that originates in your work? Explain.

4. What would your people identify as your motivation to lead? Are they right?

CHAPTER SUMMARY – Key Takeaways

* The highest correlations of motivation to lead were creating value for others, impacting change, mentoring others, personal achievement, purpose in life, and taking care of others.

* This suggests a servant-leader attitude, which is part and parcel of values-based leadership.

* Leadership is about making others become better as a result of your presence and making sure that impact lasts in your absence.

* When your motivation to lead matches those key values, you will find that your influence multiplies exponentially.

* When you lead with a higher purpose, everything around you aligns and your purpose dictates your actions.

* When we become values-based leaders and live with values at the center of our life, our motivations shift from self-serving to others-focused. The difference we make lasts long after we're gone.

CHAPTER FIVE

Leadership Styles

Leadership Style Contributes to the Success of Organizational Culture

When I first set out to discover what distinguished values-based leaders from their peers, I wanted to explore how executives' values and leadership style shaped and sustained corporate culture. Leadership style is the first external indicator of leading with values because your leadership style is something that can be chosen, and it grows and develops over time. Though leadership styles varied among the individuals I interviewed, all the leaders in the study expressed a strong desire to lead with a purpose that was bigger than themselves.

This was a key finding, as in times of fiscal stress, these leaders always turned back to the main reason why they lead in the first place and made decisions based on their higher purpose as well as their values. They also expressed the importance of being great followers.

As I mentioned previously in the book, we as leaders are often called to do something bigger than ourselves, something that requires a judgment call. Those are the moments when values show through our actions and decisions.

Ash Patel, Bank CEO, was talking to one of his key employees about his future with the company as the employee had been approached by a competitor offering more money. The employee had a wife and twins, and felt he owed his family to look into the opportunity. When Ash realized that money was the factor and taking care of his family was important to his employee, he went ahead and exceeded the salary his employee was offered somewhere else. Most people would be satisfied with that, but not Ash Patel; he said to his employee: "I'm going to continue to invest in you, and now I am also going to invest in your family." This is what he told me when I interviewed him for this book:

> *This employee has twins; I wanted to make sure he knew that I not only care about him but also about his family. So I told him that I am going to put a total of $3,000 net in a college fund account for each of his students. When I told him that, my Human Resources person told me to be cautious, as I had just promised to do this with my own personal funds. She mentioned that in order for me to do this, I would have to "gross up" the amount and it would cost me about $10,000 - $3k for each child, and in addition, taxes would have to be paid for my employee's children to get the full amount; I told her that is absolutely fine with me. I have been blessed with good fortune, and I want to share it with my employees. After that, I*

*declared that every employee's child that is born under
my leadership will get a $3,000 college fund account.*

Ash called the employee in the middle of our conversation to make sure he received the funds; I could hear the employee's wife in the background saying, "Tell your boss thank you!" During our interview Ash mentioned how he genuinely cared not only about his employees, but also about their family… He was leading with values.

> WHEN COMPETENT PEOPLE FEEL VALUED, RESPECTED AND RECOGNIZED FOR THEIR WORK, THE NUMBERS ALWAYS COME.

Leadership and values go hand in hand. I have discovered that successful leaders have alignment between their values and leadership style. While the style can vary from person to person, what is imperative is that their values play a key role in the development and execution of how they lead.

Every time I take on an assignment, I look for alignment between my values and the leadership style of the people in the organization. Like many of the leaders I interviewed, I focus on people first, and numbers second. When competent people feel valued, respected and recognized for their work, the numbers always come.

After speaking at a leadership conference in San Diego in the fall of 2015, a young woman waited patiently to meet with me. Connie Lewis explained that she worked for Heartland Payment Systems, and exclaimed that her CEO, Bob Carr, was just like me, someone who lived and led with values. "You have to meet him," she insisted. Intrigued, I agreed to meet him and gave her my contact information. I had no idea at the time, but Ms. Lewis began lobbying on my behalf, telling Bob, "You have to meet Dr. Betty Uribe!" Two weeks later I received a copy of his book titled *Through the Fires*, with a hand-written note from him acknowledging Conni's introduction. After I read his book (a must read), I knew I had to interview him for my book, so I sent an email asking for a few minutes on the phone. He was a very busy man, and the first time he was able to call was right after he had sold his company. He began our call with the words: *"I'm in NYC at the airport. I just signed papers to sell the company for $4.3 billion."* Without hesitation, I screamed, "What? And you're talking to me?" I could not believe that someone having just sold his company would take the time to chat with me about values. He replied with an easy candor, *"I thought this would be a pleasant call after signing the papers selling my company."* I smiled at his response, and then my curiosity got ahold of me. I asked him, "What's going through your mind right now?" What was going on behind the curtain in his mind? Without even thinking, he replied, *"I feel bad about my employees. They have been with me for a long time, and I want to make sure they're going to be okay."* This man had just sold the company he had been leading for some time; he was now worth more than he could have ever imagined, and his most pressing concern was for the welfare of his employees. I knew right then that I had found a kindred spirit.

My leadership style is highly collaborative, something I look for when joining a new team, be it a board of directors, a job, or a sub-committee for a larger cause. Studies show that decision quality improves significantly when a group of people collaborate to make the final decision. When I interviewed with California

Bank & Trust, a Division of Zions Bancorporation, I noticed something unique with CEO David Blackford and the Executive Management Committee reporting to him. All major bank decisions were made by the leadership team—contrary to many companies where the CEO or person in command makes all key decisions, many times without consulting their team. This team collaborated, and decisions were made by consensus or alignment. (Alignment is when not all individuals in the decision team are in favor of the decision; however, they align with the decision and support and own the decision for the good of the whole). This level of collaboration at the top of the company made my decision to join an easy one; they matched my values (people first), and my leadership style (collaborative).

In this chapter we will take a close look at the background and the importance of studying leadership styles in all areas of business. For those of you who like to learn how things came about, I will take you through a journey of the evolution of leadership theories. We will also review the literature as it examines the values and leadership characteristics of CEOs and senior executives in the field of financial services, CEOs and senior executives in business, and military generals.

Historically, culture is a key factor influencing the success and failure in an organization. However, in addition to culture, a leader's chosen leadership style also matters a great deal.[10] We simply need to look to recent history to validate this concept.

Throughout the past two decades, macroeconomic forces have forced many organizations to undergo traumatic change. In 1999 it was argued that companies that focus on people and leaders who create a culture—or social environment—where employees thrive will achieve sustainable performance.[11] As observed in recent history, many leaders and entire organizations have fallen as a result of leaders' values being compromised.

In order to get a clear view of what leaders must do to keep their organizations afloat and support the creation of an economy that thrives, it is important to learn from the past. With that in mind, the next section takes a journey through leadership theories, the three main leadership styles, and real-life examples of application of principles to encourage overall employee growth, a healthy corporate culture, and sustainable performance. Let's start with how we got here.

Evolution of Leadership Theories

While the term *leader* was listed only fairly recently by the Oxford English Dictionary in 1933, the term *leadership* has been in existence since the late 1700s.[12] The topic of leadership has come up time and time again throughout history, especially in times of rapid change. However, scientific research on the topic of leadership began in the 20th century with the pursuit of the following question:

What makes an effective leader?

Great Man Theory of Leadership

Philosophers in the 18th and 19th century proposed a leadership theory called the **Great Man Theory of Leadership**. It was believed that people were born with innate qualities and characteristics of social, political, and military leaders. This theory espoused that leaders are born with personality traits that could be used to delineate leaders from non-leaders. It emphasized traits, NOT situations. Therefore leadership was reserved for those who were "natural born leaders."

Traits and Characteristic, Power and Influence Leadership Theories

In the early 1900s, the traits and characteristic leadership theories emerged. These questioned the premise of the Great Man Theory, suggesting that perhaps leadership is not innate. Leadership factors were identified as ones that create exemplary job performance in an organization. Traits theory was most prominent between 1904 and 1947. Although this was a popular approach, empirical studies by Jenkins and Stogdill revealed no specific trait or characteristics associated with effective leadership.[13] Since most traits can't be learned, and studies resulted in no conclusive evidence, researchers moved toward the importance of *concern for people* as an effective leadership quality. However, traits have been added to more recent leadership theories[14]—although not as a focus, but more as variables in leadership theory.[15]

In 1954, a new belief emerged that one could become a stronger leader by copying these great leaders' personalities and behaviors.[16] Most recently, the *trait approach* has increased in popularity.

In 1985, it was found that most leaders or managers elicit merely competent performance from their followers, while a select few inspire extraordinary achievement. *Transformational,* or *charismatic leadership* styles emerged. This shows that the *trait approach* is still very much alive today.

After the 1940s, it was found that leadership was not only trait related, but also aspects of power and influence came to light in subsequent research. Specifically, attempts were made to explain the effectiveness of the leader by showing the amount and utilization of power. While researchers found that power influence was prevalent in leadership, the authoritarian, controlling aspects of this type of leadership were not found to be effective.[17]

Skills-Based Leadership Model

In the 1970s A new direction began to shape leadership research in which leaders' *actions* were emphasized, as opposed to their *traits* or *sources of power*. Leaders could now focus on implementing specific *actions* to improve their effectiveness as leaders. Some of the research during this time focused on analyzing *behavioral differences* between poor and effective leaders, and resulted in a *skill-based model* that was enhanced later.[18] It was found that *capabilities could be developed over time through education and experience*. Unlike the Great Man Approach, which implies that leadership is innate and cannot be learned, the skills approach suggests that *leadership is open to many people as long as they can learn from their experiences*.

This was viewed as a breakthrough in leadership, as all of a sudden, the idea of being a great leader was open to the general population, not just the privileged few.

> LEADERSHIP IS OPEN TO MANY PEOPLE AS LONG AS THEY CAN LEARN FROM THEIR EXPERIENCES.

In the 1960s, two schools of thought emerged: The X Theory and the Y Theory.[19] Theory X positioned people as passive; as a result needing to be directed and extrinsically motivated. Conversely, Theory Y stated that people are already motivated intrinsically, and hence only require the right working conditions. During this time, researchers found that it was the leaders' responsibility to provide the conditions and stimulus to evoke the right types of behaviors.[20] All of a sudden, leaders had the power to find out what motivates their people: If extrinsically motivated, the leaders could offer external factors like more money, time off, etc. for a job well done; if intrinsically motivated, the leaders could now find out what excited their employees, and provide that for them when producing desired results.

QUESTIONS TO KEEP YOU THINKING

1. Give an example of how someone you know who recently exhibited the traits cited in the Great Man Theory, which argues that leadership is innately generated.

2. Give an example how someone you know recently exhibited the traits cited in the Skills-Based Theory, which argues that leadership is learned.

3. How do you currently use Theory X in your leadership style? (People are passive and need to be directed and extrinsically motivated.) What advantages and disadvantages do you see in this approach?

4. How do you currently use Theory Y in your leadership style? (People are already intrinsically motivated and only require the right conditions to perform.) What advantages and disadvantages do you see in this approach?

Situational Leadership

The situational approach emerged and became very popular in the 1980's.[21] In this approach, the leader is flexible in style, *depending on the specific situation*. According to Blanchard and Ziganni,[22] leadership styles can be classified into four categories:

1. Directing Approach - High-directive, Low-supportive

2. Coaching Approach - High-directive, High-supportive

3. Supporting Approach - High-supportive, Low-directive

4. Delegating Approach - Low-supportive, Low-directive

In this leadership model, no one leadership style is touted as best. Like a chameleon who changes color based on their environment, effective leaders adapt their leadership style according to the situation—to match the appropriate leadership style to the individual's or group's development level.

Another type of situational leadership, **Contingency Theory** is concerned with styles and situations. Fred Fiedler developed the **Leader-Match Theory**, with which leaders are matched appropriately to the situations. The theory is called "contingency" because it depends on how well the leader's style matches the context. From time to time in my career, I have employed executive coaches to support the growth of some of my senior leaders. I recently had the opportunity to choose an executive coach for one of my new senior managers. I interviewed many people and finally chose someone who matched the culture, background, and style of the leader. This was a great success, as their personalities matched, and there was instant credibility. Had

I chosen a person with a style that didn't match the individual, it could have been disastrous.

As I interviewed the study participants, they were very open in sharing their respective leadership styles. Several were able to point to examples of situational leadership that they had utilized in their careers.

Vice Admiral Raquel C. Bono of the US Navy described a situation where she had to act with integrity despite the negative consequences that would undoubtedly arise:

> When I was in Jacksonville, I was getting ready to welcome a new executive officer who happened to be a wonderful personal friend. Unfortunately, she had a weight problem, and it became apparent that she would not make the weight standards required of an executive officer. She showed up, and immediately 4,000 people were talking about it. I knew that we are in the business of war and an officer must be within weight standards. I was faced with the decision to remedy the situation while creating the opportunity to maintain dignity and self-respect. Though I was angry that the situation had not been caught before this very important promotion, I had to stick to my guns and do what was right and what was expected from the senior leaders who were the biggest change agents and watching very closely. The end result was that I gave her the option of staying, but I said that she couldn't be an executive officer. I took a lot of grief from people in other areas, but the entire command would have taken a bullet for me. That situation underlined the

cold, hard reality of military standards and she paid the price with senior leadership. A captain called me to ask why I made that decision, and I answered that I couldn't ask an enlistee to do something that my own leadership team was unable to do. It's about integrity.

QUESTIONS TO KEEP YOU THINKING

1. Which of the situational leadership categories do you most relate to?

    i. Directing Approach - High-directive, Low-supportive

    ii. Coaching Approach - High-directive, High-supportive

    iii. Supporting Approach - High-supportive, Low-directive

    iv. Delegating Approach - Low-supportive, Low-directive

2. Which situational leadership category is most effective in times of fiscal change? Explain.

3. Describe a situation where you have been stretched to change your natural style to create better results.

    i. What was the situation?

    ii. What style did you change to that is different than your natural style?

    iii. What were the results?

    iv. What did you learn?

The two most contemporary theoretical models are *transactional* and *transformational.*

Transactional Leadership Theory

In the **transactional** leadership model, subordinates are rewarded for completing required tasks and punished for failing to complete the same. These transactional rewards can be: (a) Promotions, (b) Praise, and (c) Monetary compensation. Although these rewards are clearly identified, negative consequences such as undesirable feedback and reproof still loom large. Most relationships between leader and subordinate fall under transactional, where the leaders and subordinates expect an exchange for the work done.

Study participants cited three different segments of transactional leadership that they utilized in their roles as senior executives:

1. Directed (micro-management)

2. Lead by Example

3. Manage by Objectives.

Only one of the executives admitted to micromanaging employees, and he had this to say of directed leadership:

> *I take my time selecting the people, give them their goals, and let them go to see how they perform. However, I'm not very tolerant of mistakes. I feel like if I give the opportunity and if they fail, I will be looking over their shoulder the rest of the way. If there are errors, I micro-manage people to death. People don't like that. It would be very difficult to lead if my staff didn't understand the scope of the work we do.*

What the right index finger does impacts the thumb on the left hand.

Many of the leaders expressed their desire to lead by example. Albert Schweitzer says: *"Example is not the main thing in influencing others in Transactional Leadership. It is the only thing."* Yet leading by example is something that every one of the participants understand as vital to effective leadership.

A Vice Chair for a major national banking institution says that he learned to motivate people in different ways and strove to get them to believe in the activity he desired of them:

> *Being a banker is about solving financial problems and enabling the process of resolution for our clients. I lead by example for my leaders by getting to know my people, and participating in the process of bringing new customers to the bank by going out and meeting with prospective clients instead of leading from my office. Whatever I do as the leader, I need to be engaged with my employees so they believe in the activities I ask from them and develop a feeling a value.*

General Mick Kicklighter of the US Army described a situation where he had to be tough and expected his people to adhere to high standards:

> *When I took command of the 25th division, the vice chief of staff of the army called me in and said, "Mick, you're taking command of a division that's got the worst aviation safety record in the army and if you don't correct the problem, your command tour is going to be very short." Even though I didn't create*

the problem, I had a mission to solve it. My answer? High standards. When I arrived in Hawaii, I told the division, "All safety in this division is going to be the best. We're going to train hard and we're going to do whatever it takes to be combat ready, but we are not going to have any accidents if we can possibly prevent it, and that includes aviation. They knew that if they didn't enforce the policies I put into place, they'd have to deal with me. I think it was because I believed it could be done. They began to believe it could be done as well. Almost overnight our aviation safety record went from the worst to the best.

Vice Admiral Raquel C. Bono of the US Navy says of negotiating personnel issues with high standards:

I strive to understand why people aren't able to do what I'm asking them to do and find out their needs so I can help. Most of the time, people want to do what you're asking of them. If there are barriers, it is my job to take them away. In performance evaluations, I knew that my integrity was on the line. If someone failed their personal fitness test twice, I had the option to get them out. It's not my desire to ruin anyone's opportunity, but it's my intention to ensure everyone is held accountable. I hold myself to the very same standard. My nickname is "Rocky" (because I never give up)—if I can take a group of people that don't work for me and get them in alignment enough that they make change happen, that's leadership!

I agree 100 percent, Raquel!

QUESTIONS TO KEEP YOU THINKING

1. What aspects of your leadership style are more transactional? Explain.

2. What do you think about Albert Schweitzer's saying that "example is not the main thing in influencing others—it is the only thing"? Why or why not?

3. In the last week, what situations do you recall when you or your immediate manager led by example? What about when they didn't?

4. What lessons did you gain from this section?

Transformational Leadership Theory

Giving unconditionally! Is there such a thing as giving to your people and leading them without expecting anything in return? ANYTHING? Not even a simple "Thank you?" The transformational leader looks to engage the follower without regard for any transactional exchange. Such a leader might introduce into the organization, a mission, vision, and values for the purpose of instilling pride in the organization *without expecting anything in return* for his or her leadership.

Transformational leadership was first introduced in 1978:[23] "*A context in which the leader and the follower engage in such a way that both are raised to a level of motivation that is higher than it would have been without such engagement.*" This level of engagement causes employer and employee to create deeper bonds with one another.

Transformational leadership manifested through four different management styles:

1. Collaborative

2. Listening leader

3. Open door/inclusive

4. Servant leader

Collaborative Leader

Collaborative leaders are engaged with their team and have the credibility to bring together the right people to create visions and solve problems.[24] General Dwight D. Eisenhower was known to possess the spirit of collaboration. To collaborate effectively, leaders must be *humble, patient,* and *flexible* to gain the confidence of their colleagues. Like Eisenhower, the leader with cross-cultural strengths recognizes the importance of *accountability, humility, flexibility, consultation, patience,* and *trust.*

> SOMETIMES YOU'RE DEALT A HAND AND YOU'VE GOT TO PLAY IT, YOU HAVE NO CHOICE .

It must be noticed that every one of the leaders highlighted in this book mentioned that women have a higher tendency to collaborate. Women can nurture and build teams while maintaining a high motivation to succeed. They are collaborative, good at building consensus, natural multitaskers, and able to wear different hats effectively.

General Mick Kicklighter of the US Army has decades of experience leading and developing men and women on his team, but it has not always been easy.

I always try to look for a core group of people that I can rely on, but it doesn't always happen. Sometimes you're dealt a hand and you've got to play it, you have no choice. This is your team. Ideally, you want to build a core of very competent, very dedicated, and very professional people that you know would move heaven and earth to get the job done. When I have been given the option to choose my team, I have select those people who are rock solid, will stay the course, and will do whatever has to be done.

Isn't that what you want on your team as well?

Effective leaders are engaged leaders, who build upon the strengths of their team.

Listening Leader

The listening transformational leader is really an extension of the collaborative leadership style. An effective listener nurtures an environment of inclusivity. You've already heard how one of the leaders intentionally met with every single manager in his first 100 days on the job. Why? To be in the trenches with them, listen to them, and build trust with them.

Lynn Carter, president of Capital One Bank at the time of my interview, says this of leading with a collaborative, listening leader style:

Some people said I was too open, too willing to listen to what others had to say or what they thought. However, I believe that the crowd is a powerful force. If you're not open to listening, you close yourself off to opportunities.

I absolutely love the diversity of experience and thought represented by my team. I work hard to make sure that atmosphere of listening is always there.

Maria Salinas utilizes a listening, empathetic leadership style when meeting with her board.

I have sixteen board members that I meet with two times a week, and I always ask everyone their opinion before sharing mine. I intentionally acknowledge everything they have to say and mirror back their responses to show that I hear and understand them.

By allowing her team to share their opinions before she shares hers, the team is free to share their own opinion without being influenced by their leader; as a result, the leader gets honest feedback. Sometimes being a listening leader means that you're going to hear things you don't want to hear.

Open Door Inclusive Leader

According to Edwin Hollander's work, *Inclusive Leadership*,[25] the inclusive transformational leader does things *with* people rather than *to* people. He states that inclusive leadership respects confrontation and cooperation as part of creating a healthy participative process.

Former president of Capital One Bank Lynn Carter knows all about the leader-follower dynamic and believes it begins with trust:

It all starts with trust. Trust is paramount to having integrity and respect. How do you build trust? You do what you say with honesty, openness, and you put your cards on the table. I encourage open dialogue as well as open conflict because you cannot be afraid to confront the tough stuff. Some of the most trusting relationships I've built have been off the back of tough conversations. You make it about the issue, not the person, and it turns into a growth experience.

That type of open-door leadership is the kind that encourages buy-in and engagement from the leader-follower relationship. It perfectly leads into the last style of transformational leadership exhibited by those in my study: servant leadership.

Servant Leadership

I shared in chapter one of this book my definition of servant leadership: *Leaders whose actions are aligned with their espoused values. They lead with integrity, focus on the good of the whole, and make a positive impact in others.* It's not necessarily just about serving others. It's about selflessness; it's more aligned with the military model of a leader, being congruent, and putting their troops and their families first.

Coined by Robert K. Greenleaf in 1970, the characterization of a servant-leader focuses primarily on the growth and well-being of people and the communities to which they belong. While traditional leadership generally involves the accumulation and exercise of power by one at the "top of the pyramid," servant leadership is different. The servant-leader in the context of this book doesn't focus on *keeping* the power; instead they *share* the power; they put the needs of others first and focus on helping people develop and perform to their full potential. This is a key distinction as most leaders today confuse power with EMpower.

Servant leaders EMpower their people and are not intimidated, but rather re-energized when they get the opportunity to lead others who may be stronger than them in one way or another.

One of the leaders who models this particularly well is Bob Carr. He was President and CEO of Heartland Payments at the time of the interview. When I asked previous employees to comment on Bob, everyone showed such care; it was as if they personally knew him, although some of them were in remote places and had never even met Bob in person. I was so impressed with the comments that I made it a point to consult with current employees. Here's what Connie Moore Lewis said:

> *Bob led by example; he always used his personal experiences in life to offer others a better place to work and raise our family. His goal was to produce a workplace where people liked to come to work. He always made us feel like an equal.*
>
> *Bob regularly surveyed his employees to find out what they liked and what they didn't like about their jobs. Bob would talk about the results, reading the bad comments as well as the good ones at our annual meeting. When Heartland won top workplace award in the USA, Bob mentioned that was his biggest accomplishment.*

This leader understood that once his people knew that he truly cared about them, they would be inspired by his vision and hence their trust factor increased greatly. Trust translates to happiness and overall satisfaction. Greg Jacobson says it this way: "I believe the mood or state of mind of happiness is fundamentally unselfish.

Yes, you're the one feeling it, but usually it occurs because you're involved with something more than just yourself. In studying happiness, I've found that it must benefit the greater good, or it's unsustainable and short-lived."

Lessons Learned

As leaders we are called upon to inspire others to follow our lead and walk alongside with us on a journey that is bigger than us—this journey can't be accomplished well, without the collaboration of groups of people with similar values, vision and purpose. This happens easily when we first focus on our people. When trust is built, results come faster because there is no wasted time in politics, and people second-guessing what the leader could be up to; instead everyone works together for the good of the whole. Communication and transparency are key. Like Bob Carr, who chose transparency for his employees and shareholders in the midst of one of the biggest security breaches in the history of the industry, it is our duty as leaders to lead with transparency, honesty, communication and collaboration. It is only then that we are able to build values-centered teams who carry the same values, vision and purpose, and create sustainable high results where everyone wins.

QUESTIONS TO KEEP YOU THINKING

1. What is your leadership style and how do you create trust in your organization? Give examples from your own experience.

    i. Collaborative

      ii. Listener

      iii. Open Door

      iv. Servant Leader

2. After reading the stories and examples of the leaders who were interviewed,

      i. What takeaways will help you inject values in your organization?

      ii. How will you ensure trust is built in sustained in your organization?

      iii. How will you ensure your people feel valued and heard?

3. Explain how you will implement at least one tenet of transformational leadership in your organization or in your day-to-day life.

Transformational leadership may be the key to unlocking the hidden potential of your team. Creating and maintaining a positive organizational culture is a common ingredient of successful organizations, and your chosen leadership style matters to your company culture. Going back to the question of "What makes an effective leader?" that sparked the original and ongoing research into leadership, it all comes down to the bottom line of profitability, which is entirely quantifiable. Yet a better, more qualitative, question may be this:

Is your organization growing, thriving, and producing new leaders?

Your leadership style should most certainly include the continual development and growth of the next generation of effective leaders. Values-based leaders who focus on people first create organizations where employees thrive and achieve sustainable performance.

CHAPTER SUMMARY – Key Takeaways

- Companies that focus on people first create an environment where employees thrive and achieve sustainable high performance.

- The evolution of leadership theories progressed as follows: Great Man Theory, Traits and Characteristics Theories, and Skills-based models.

- The three modern styles of leadership are Situational, Transactional, and Transformational.

- Directed, Lead by Example, and Manage by Objectives are three types of transactional leadership.

- Three styles of Transformational Leadership: Collaborative, Listening, Open-door/Inclusive, and Servant leaders.

- Trust is critical to building high performing teams.

- Trust is built by listening to your employees, getting to know them and creating active processes of communication where employees are free to speak their mind without fear of retaliation.

CHAPTER SIX

Overcoming Obstacles

***The obstacles a person faces serve as stepping
stones for personal and leadership development.***

*"One who gains strength by overcoming obstacles possesses the
only strength which can overcome adversity."*
—Albert Schweitzer

Everyone faces obstacles. If we're honest, we face them every day. The question is not do we face obstacles; the question is what do we do with them. Situations that test your perseverance and stretch you to the breaking point are exceptionally instrumental in your growth.

Former CEO and author of *Discovering Your True North*, Bill George, speaks to this idea when he talks about crucible moments—those moments in our lives that ultimately work to define us.[26] In his book, he shares stories of the best and brightest leaders and how their crucible moments molded them into the people they became. George uses the analogy of how an oyster pearl is formed. When sand grates against an oyster, its natural reaction is to cover the sand to protect itself, thereby forming the pearl. Without the irritant of the sand, the beautiful pearl would never be fashioned. When we look at the obstacles and trials in our lives as potential crucible moments, we can turn any difficult, painful experience into an opportunity for growth.

I remember one difficult situation in my career that taught me an important lesson about seeing an obstacle as an opportunity to learn. When I first started with Wells Fargo almost three decades ago, I had a manager who made it clear to me that nothing was good enough for him. I had never worked for a bank before, so I called up the number one person and learned everything I could, soaking in their secrets about how they got to be the best. I worked hard and became the number one banker in Southern California in my first six months. Not good enough for him. One day I had heart palpitations and felt that I needed to go to the hospital, he wouldn't let me go. Seriously.

Instead of reacting with disdain and giving up on him, I thought to myself, *I'm going to invest the time in getting to know him.* Even though I lived in Carlsbad and worked in El Toro—a one to one-and-one-half-hour commute each way—I would stay late just so I could talk to him about his children and his life. He really was a grouchy old man! Yet because I took the time to get to know the person behind the "grouchy old man" mask, I was finally able to build trust with him and eventually he actually trusted and respected me. Fast forward several years, and I ended up managing a group of branches, and one of them was his branch. We even won a trip to Hawaii as a group of branches, and we eventually became good friends.

I could have given up and written off the grouchy manager as a lost cause. Yet I chose to view my very unpleasant obstacle as an opportunity to learn, and I persevered through it to create a relationship that has lasted to this day. Through this relationship, I learned patience, learned not to judge but to ask questions and actively listen for queues that would give me insight into what made him tick, and I learned the art of communication. I took the time to really get to know him; I learned about his children, his family, and his hobby as a DJ which was very important to him. He felt that I valued who HE was, and in return, he began to trust and respect me and we ended up having a great working relationship built on trust and respect for one another. But I took the time. I didn't give up on him.

Our obstacles and crucible moments teach us invaluable life and leadership lessons and uniquely prepare us for our journey—only if we are willing to see them as such.

Founder and CEO of Heartland Payment Systems Inc. Bob Carr shared his view of obstacles and how they figure into success:

> *If you have a well-thought-out plan and you stick to it and keep modifying it as you learn new things, it can be incredibly powerfully successful. That's the Heartland story. I started out with a model that made sense to me and kept running into one detour or roadblock or another, like anyone else. As you figure out how to get around those roadblocks, you're figuring out how to solve the problems that everybody else tries to solve, yet few are successful at doing. You become an "overnight success" after forty-three years.*

In a 2007 blog post by Paul Coehlo, best-selling author of the novel *The Alchemist,* shares the account of a butterfly emerging from its cocoon, adapted from a story by Sonaira D'Avila. Coehlo reveals how a man watches a butterfly struggling to emerge from its cocoon and eventually intervenes:

> A man spent hours watching a butterfly struggling to emerge from its cocoon. It managed to make a small hole, but its body was too large to get through it. After a long struggle, it appeared to be exhausted and remained absolutely still. The man decided to help the butterfly and, with a pair of scissors, he cut open the cocoon, thus releasing the butterfly. However, the butterfly's body was very small and wrinkled and its wings were all crumpled. The man continued to watch, hoping that, at any moment, the butterfly would open its wings and fly away. Nothing happened; in fact, the butterfly spent the rest of its brief life dragging around its shrunken body and shriveled wings, incapable of flight. What the man – out of kindness and his eagerness to help – had failed to understand was that the tight cocoon and the efforts that the butterfly had to make in order to squeeze out of that tiny hole were nature's way of training the butterfly and of strengthening its wings.[27]

We can view our obstacles in the same way. The very circumstances that seem to stretch us to our breaking points may be the very situations that refine us, develop us, and transform us— strengthening our wings and preparing us for flight.

REFLECTION MOMENT

Take a moment to think about your life. You've no doubt had moments where you felt like that butterfly, exhausted and spent, fighting with your life to simply survive the struggle. You felt the relief of a hard-fought battle being over, and you had a sense that you emerged a different person because of it. Those moments are your crucibles—those things that you've faced that have become defining moments for you in your life and career.

The high-level executives and military leaders I interviewed responded with personal obstacles they experienced. One CEO shared how he was betrayed by a family member and former business partner who was even so bold as to knock off his company name, changing only one word. Others shared their struggles with feeling like an outsider or butting up against contrary ideals. The common threads expressed throughout the interviews were in the following areas: alignment of goals, bias, daunting assignments, finances, and lack of foresight. I'm certain that you will relate to some of the stories they shared.

Remember: The true test of a leader is not coming through an obstacle unscathed—it is coming through a challenging situation with the scars and bruises of insight, borne of the blood, sweat, and tears of experience.

To paraphrase Robert Frost, "The only way out is through."

Obstacles: Alignment of Goals

We have already talked about how important alignment of your values is for effective leadership, and I shared how important it is for me to work with people who have alignment with my values and leadership style. You know how vital proper alignment is for something as down-to-earth as your car—without the right alignment, your car will burn through more fuel, tires will experience more wear and tear, and even such systems as your suspension and breaking system can decrease in effectiveness. All of this costs money to repair, while a proper alignment could have avoided all of that in the first place.

In the same way, effective leaders should build alignment in values and goals. Even if one system is out of alignment, the damage can be vast and unmitigated. Lynn Carter, former president of Capital One Bank, experienced this misalignment firsthand, and it became a significant career obstacle:

> *The toughest times in my career were when I was in an environment that didn't support my values, which are team-building, trust, respect, and constructive relationships. I found myself around folks who cared more about their own personal well-being than the well-being of the team and who had a lack of respect for the experience of others and how that could make the business better. I've even worked with people whom I did not respect because of their actions, and I've worked with people who have done things that I felt were unethical and unbecoming and dishonest. The toughest is when you see somebody make a mistake that is so bad, so egregious, that you really have to take action and deal with it. When they were my senior, as they were in some cases, it was difficult to have to live through that and deal with it. When they were*

my subordinates, it was also very hard to deal with because there was only one choice. I couldn't look the other way or pretend it didn't happen. I had to take action with people I loved like family, but you do what you know is right.

In a more general sense, CEO Matt Toledo of the LA Business Journal feels the disparity of character when working with those who display a misalignment with his values:

I've made a very clear decision to distance myself from people of lesser character. I use my judgment to determine what the right conduct is for any given situation, and those are the voices I honor and carry forward. I just immediately erase the negative voices from the essence of who I am because I don't want to give them the space or the oxygen to flourish. I've made a life of distancing myself from people who are not of good character and surrounding myself with people who have displayed good values and judgment.

Obstacles: Bias

Unfortunately, despite moving forward in many respects, there still exists in our modern society a stronghold of bias rooted in variances of gender, ethnicity, and financial status, among others. Most of the study participants who mentioned bias as a major career obstacle were women in the military who, despite their high position, intelligence, and capability, encountered gender bias on the job. US Marine Corps Major General Angie Salinas shared her struggles as she assumed a position where 99 percent of the retirees were male:

Every time I went into a position as the first woman, it was challenging because there was no mark, no standard to measure against—only that of a male. Anything that was different became an obstacle to overcome. Despite their doubts, I knew I was the best qualified general to be there, so I had to be much more conscientious in proving myself.

US Navy Command Surgeon Vice Admiral Raquel C. Bono shared a similar experience with gender bias:

Discrimination for me has come in the form of not being respected. You can see it in their eyes when they don't take you seriously. I'm short, tiny, and some find me cute. I'm also athletic, like to be in shape, and I love to wow people when they realize I'm good at what I do. Women have to work 2-3-4 times as hard, especially in the surgical field.

Gender bias is obviously not exclusive to the military, however. Chairwoman of ProAmerica Bank, Maria Salinas, shared how both her ethnicity and gender gave her a sense of being the only one (the only woman, the only Latina) early on in her accounting career and in the corporate arena.

When I was with Disney in the corporate environment, it hit me the hardest because not only was I the only Latina on the team, I was the only female at the manager level. It was definitely a culture that was not as inclusive as it should have been. That was extremely difficult for me. One of the things that I learned is that you can't give up. There were a lot of times where I felt like I wanted to give up and just go work somewhere else. I think I came out the stronger person for persevering, for having gone through something like that. Today, I feel like I can have a stronger, more confident voice. I feel very proud about my experience. I got here because I earned it.

Like the butterfly, Maria Salinas persevered through the obstacles that she faced, rather than giving up, and emerged a stronger person with a more confident voice. She leveraged the experience of that crucible moment into invaluable personal and professional growth. She chose to see her struggle as an opportunity to become better, more effective as an individual and a leader.

Obstacles: Daunting Assignments

Perhaps one of the best leaders to discuss daunting assignments in their career is Retired US Army General Mick Kicklighter, who has been asked to serve in some of the most challenging missions, some originating directly from the Secretary of Defense at the time, Donald Rumsfeld. I shared part of the story in the chapter on strengths, but the whole story is detailed below:

One December Friday night in 2003, my wife Betty and I were sitting at home when I got a call from Secretary Don Rumsfeld's office. At the time, I was serving as the Assistant Secretary for Policy Planning and Preparedness in the Department of Veteran Affairs. The secretary wanted to see me the next morning at 9 am, and they were not at liberty to convey any details. It turned out to be the morning they had captured the former president of Iraq, Saddam Hussein, and there were only three other people in the room when Secretary Rumsfeld and I finally met around 10:30 am. After some pleasantries, he conveyed that I had been recommended for a mission to aid in returning sovereignty to Iraq on a much shorter timeline—by June of 2004, only a few short months away.

He asked about my career and what I had accomplished. Apparently satisfied with what he heard, he told me, "Well, this is the mission. We've got to put a team together that can devise a plan to close down the Coalition Provision Authority which Ambassador Bremer is running. At the same time, we have to plan to return the sovereignty of the Iraqi people and put a US Embassy in place. Do you think that you're capable of leading an effort like that?" I had to really sit back and think about it, but responded with, "Yes, sir, I can." It was a very daunting task all the way from the beginning to the end, requiring a tremendous amount of work and responsibility. The mission necessitated a very comprehensive, detailed plan to make it happen, but we made the transition two days earlier than the deadline and caught everyone by surprise, including the media and Al-Qaeda.

You will most certainly face daunting assignments in your life and career, whether you are a CEO, Head of State, General in the Military, Executive, Manager, Coach, Teacher, Accountant, Mother, Father, Salesperson, or in any role you play in your life and career. The key to success in those assignments is understanding both your capabilities and those of the people around you. Just as General Kicklighter assembled a team whom he trusted with his life, you can surround yourself with people who support your mission, whatever outcome you seek.

One important lesson I personally learned about obstacles and daunting assignments came during a very difficult time in my life. I was going through a divorce when I received the letter of acceptance to Pepperdine University's Executive MBA program, just one week before I was to start. At the time, I faced the reality that I was going to be a single parent to two small daughters ages two and four. I thought to myself, *I cannot go to graduate school now.* Feeling beaten down and overwhelmed by my circumstances, I went to my best friend for advice. She encouraged me with words that I will never forget:

"Don't ever let anyone take anything away from you. You will figure out how to make it happen."

I didn't let anyone take my dream away from me, and I hold that truth with me to this day. I finished at the top of my graduating class, but my path was not full of roses and rainbows. One particular day I, again, felt overwhelmed by my circumstances and the sheer weight of my responsibilities, both academic, personal, and professional. I asked to meet with my strategy professor – we called him "Bubba" at 7:30 am to discuss my concerns. The moment I started to talk to him, I broke down. This was huge, because I was so very private. I confessed to him, "I don't know that I can make this assignment." He said to me, "Betty, don't worry about the assignment—you tell me when you are able to turn it in." So I set myself up to win by giving myself a later deadline, but finished the assignment on time after all. The fact that he believed in me and was willing to bend the rules spoke volumes to me about his faith in me as a student and as a person.

Sometimes it just takes one person coming alongside to give you the courage and confidence to know that you can overcome whatever you're facing.

I also learned that it never hurts to ask for things. I have had so many people tell me over the last few years, "We've never done this before," and "Wow, you're the first one who has asked for that." Yet because I asked, I have been granted the opportunity to do some amazing things like being honored as a delegate of the Colombian-American Embassy in Washington, D.C., representing Colombians abroad and visiting with President Uribe at the White House in Colombia where we actually got to plan with him some strategies for Colombians Abroad. I also got to participate in a very exclusive weekly meeting where leaders from the Presidential Palace in Colombia and the Pentagon meet regularly to discuss leadership issues—I have an open door invitation for life to this one! I've spoken in Asia as keynote speaker for the Maple Women's Society's twentieth-year anniversary, one year after Hilary Clinton was their keynote. These are just a few examples of how just anyone with the right attitude, leadership style and desire to be of service, can get to places by merely asking: "Can I go?" More on this later.

Obstacles: Financial

So many CEOs and finance executives have fallen to the siren song of a quick profit and lost their integrity in the process. After the key economic downturns between 1987 and 2007, it has become even more critical to understand the importance of values-centered leadership. In times of fiscal stress, studies have shown that values-based companies thrive where others fall apart. How? Their leaders understand their role in emphasizing safety and security (Maslow's basic needs) and how they are critical for their organization to be free to produce, innovate, problem solve, and accept the facts, in order to overcome obstacles related with any economic downturn.

Former president of Capital One Bank Lynn Carter echoes those thoughts:

> *I have an eternal optimism so anytime I am challenged, I look at the obstacle as an opportunity. We as leaders need to take full accountability for the environment not being what it needs to be and change it. We are in the driver's seat—we don't have to stay in that environment. Even if an environment is not fixable, you walk away from those situations with the mindset that it was not a failure; you have simply finished your work there. This kind of mindset brings such a sense of purpose, both for yourself and your team.*

The only way out is through. That means you have the power to change your circumstances if they are not working. Sometimes that means doing the work you can and having the courage to walk away with purpose when your work is done.

Obstacles: Lack of Foresight

Hindsight is 20/20 as the saying goes, and we have all experienced the feeling of knowing that we missed our goals, handled a situation without enough preparation, or simply lacked the tools or details to engage effectively with a problem. Maria Salinas, Chairwoman of the Board for ProAmerica bank at the time, shared that she wished that she had gone to graduate school, but added that it's not too late in her career to do so and she still considers that possibility. Though she has accomplished so much in her career from finance to the corporate world and gained invaluable experiences in each position she has held, she still recognizes the potential and value of higher education. I'm reminded of General Kicklighter's and Lynn Carter's words that they would "never stop learning." That drive to learn and grow can prove to be a tremendously effective vehicle for overcoming obstacles. Each time you overcome something that is difficult and daunting, as General Kicklighter did in Iraq, you gain the experience and real-world knowledge that will see you through the next seemingly impossible challenge.

QUESTIONS TO KEEP YOU THINKING

1. Take a moment to think of the biggest obstacles you've experienced in your life and career.

    a. How did you handle the obstacle?

    b. What did you learn?

    c. What will you do differently as a result of what you learned so far?

2. How were the obstacles you cited in question #1 opportunities for growth in your career?

3. How has you education supported your professional growth efforts? Explain.

Though they faced a myriad of career obstacles, either self-imposed or externally initiated, these leaders always looked for a way to overcome them. Some saw obstacles as an opportunity, while others saw them as just something to get past: The only way out is through.

Whatever your view on obstacles, as a leader you have the choice to face each one with values at the core of your thinking and decision making. Even when dealing with obstacles, you can be a leader whose actions are congruent with your espoused values, one who leads with integrity, focuses on the good of the whole, and makes a positive impact on others.

QUESTIONS TO KEEP YOU THINKING

1. What is the biggest challenge or issue you are encountering in your life right now? Make an action plan of how you can address these issues with values at the center.

2. What is your strategy for getting people aligned with your vision and goals?

3. How can you ensure the alignment is sustainable in your organization?

CHAPTER SUMMARY – Key Takeaways

* Obstacles do not have to be seen as purely negative. They can be seen as opportunities for growth and learning.

* Effective leaders create alignment in values and purpose in order to succeed.

* Interview participants listed five obstacles they faced in their careers: alignment of goals, daunting assignments, finances, bias, and lack of foresight.

* Values-based leaders can tackle and overcome obstacles while still keeping their actions congruent with their values, leading with integrity, focusing on the good of the whole, and making a positive impact on others.

CHAPTER SEVEN

In the Trenches

*Military leadership values and principles can
lend themselves well to civilian organizations*

*"Leadership is a potent combination of strategy and character.
But if you must be without one, be without strategy."*
— US Army 4-Star General Norman Schwarzkopf
(Stormin' Norman)

While the civilian world does not contain the blasting sounds of mortar fire or the actual threat of danger to one's comrades, there are certainly situations in which leaders are faced with the opportunity to utilize their values in order to overcome very real obstacles.

The truth is, you go into battle each and every day.

Your battlefield is your competition, and your colleagues your comrades. Each time you wake up and begin your daily tasks of answering emails, endless meetings, dealing with corporate, customer or employee issues, and making tough decisions, you might feel as if you should be wearing full combat gear. You will undoubtedly handle multiple skirmishes, including both enemy and friendly fire, and you must lead your team to victory. Just as the military prepares its soldiers for battle through physical, mental, and social skills development, you must condition yourself to focus on your team and train your people to make the right decisions despite any obstacles.

At one point in my career, I was leading part of a merger that seemed more like a hostile takeover. My part was to take over part of the organization, and a very small group of us orchestrated this coup. A small group of us collaborated and put together the whole plan, and we took over the organization as planned. Unbeknownst to us, on the day we took over, the other company put a "poison pill" in the organization we were taking over. In essence, they spread the message: "They're bad; we're good." I found out from one of their employees when I called one of the offices, that they were "taking everything away." We proceeded to call people, who were frantically asking, "What do we do?" I calmly reassured them, "We're going to do the right thing. We're going to show them who we are through our actions." In the midst of chaos, my leadership team focused on connecting with the people—one person at a time—letting them know they would be okay and that we would take care of them. We re-built trust with the group little by little, one person at a time. It took some time, but eventually our efforts paid off. The employees of the other organization slowly began to join our company and became our raving fans, who joined our efforts in bringing everyone else on board.

Mission accomplished.

How did we do it? We led with courage, honor, transparency and integrity. We led with our values and demonstrated them with our actions. It took much patience, communication, collaboration, authenticity, and care.

Our mission was to stabilize the teams, earn their trust, win their hearts, and finally inspire them to earn the customer's trust so they would bring their business to us. Mission accomplished. I used my turnaround model to make that happen.

Major General Angie Salinas used a similar tactic when she was asked to lead an organization in San Diego where no one knew her, and few people wanted her. She got to know her peers, her community, and her platoon members and leaders, one person at a time. Eventually she became very popular in the Military, and in her community where she was honored for making such a difference. But this is not only her story; this is the story of many of the leaders in this book, who have taken the "ground cover" approach to leadership, as opposed to "air cover." This requires dedication to everyone in the organization, and a genuine care for everyone on our team. I realize this is an old cliché, but it's so perfect for this place in this chapter: "People don't care how much you know until they know how much you care" (Author Unknown). We must show our people beyond a shadow of a doubt, that we sincerely care; whether you are leading a country where people want to know you are walking in their shoes and voicing their voice, or a company, or a movie studio. "You must know your audience and slow down enough to mold yourself to them" (Gary Kalagian).

I have a deep respect for the armed forces of the United States of America. These are men and women of high moral character and integrity and the drive to get the job done, no matter the consequences or the cost, even if that means giving up one's life to save another. Knowing and understanding the impact the military can have on its citizens and the world is one reason why I included several high-level military leaders in my study. I looked for similarities in the ways that leadership is established and developed in military ranks compared to the business and sectors. I found that the values the military introduces to each enlistee and develops throughout their career are highly applicable to *every* leader, military or otherwise. In my experience, I have seen firms across America actively recruiting military personnel because of their unique training that develops leaders and lifelong learners.

The United States armed forces place a great emphasis on leadership training for military cadets and officers from all four U.S. service academies. Officers are expected to exercise leadership skills that are aligned with a defined set of values and fundamental to their purpose and function as leaders.

It is no coincidence that many individuals who are considered to be the most significant leaders in our history served in the armed forces sometime in their career. In his book *Military Leadership: In Pursuit of Excellence*, Robert L. Taylor argues that the major differences between leaders in the military and leaders in other areas such as business, financial services, political, religious, and social organizations, sports organizations, and the like, are how they measure the bottom line. In the military, the bottom line can actually be the number of lives saved, versus the amount of revenue a company brings in the private sector.

Critical aspects of military leadership have been studied for years. In their book *The Art of Command: Military Leadership from George Washington to Colin Powell*, Harry S. Laver and Jeffrey

Matthews highlight military leaders while citing nine themes or values expressed by role models in the military: integrity, persistence, institutional leadership that delivers effectiveness and efficiency, cooperation, charismatic/inspirational leadership, visionary, technologically savvy, adaptability and effective followership.

Using General George Washington as a role model, Laver and Matthews argue that true leaders understand the value and power of establishing a reputation of integrity. This reputation supports the leader in developing trust in his or her organization, which is an important ingredient for leaders, especially when leading in tough times. In his book, *It's Your Ship: Management Techniques from the Best Damn Ship in the Navy*, Captain D. Michael Abrashoff wrote this about trust:

> *Trust is like a bank account; you have got to keep making deposits if you want it to grow. On occasion, things will go wrong, and you will have to make a withdrawal. Meanwhile, it is sitting in the bank earning interest.*

Laver and Matthews also offered General Ulysses S. Grant as a role model for his relentless resolve to achieve critical objectives, which underscores the importance of leaders needing to have unwavering determination to get the job done. Although generals must face tough times, it is during those tough times that leaders develop the inner strength and determination to complete the mission. Other leaders were featured for their leadership contributions, including Dwight D. Eisenhower for his spirit of collaboration, General Lewis B. (Chestey) Puller for his charisma and inspirational leadership, and Lieutenant General Harold G.

(Hal) Moore for his adaptability due to his intellect, courage and determination——three character traits cited by philosopher of war Carl von Clausewitz as the components necessary to adapt in the "unpredictable environment of combat." Moore bridged theory and practice throughout his career. The underlying assumption that can be deduced from records of his life was that his thirst for knowledge enabled him to be innovative and create outside-the-box strategies, which ultimately earned him the reputation as one of the most innovative tacticians in the army.[28]

To collaborate effectively, leaders must be humble, patient, and flexible to gain the confidence of their colleagues. Like Eisenhower, the leader with cross-cultural strengths recognizes the importance of accountability, humility, flexibility, consultation, patience, and trust. Treating people from other nations as equals is a clear part of cross-cultural leadership.

A charismatic leader is one who exudes inspiration, one who excites and influences followers individually and emotionally. These leaders develop a clear vision for the future, identify ambitious goals and objectives, and inspire others to follow that vision through motivation, direction, and support to reach those goals.

LEADERS IN THE MILITARY MUST LEARN TO BE GREAT FOLLOWERS BEFORE THEY WILL BE TRUSTED TO TAKE ON LEADERSHIP ROLES; EVEN IN THE HIGHEST RANKINGS AS LEADERS, THEY ARE VIEWED BY THEIR SUPERIORS AS GREAT FOLLOWERS.

Laver and Matthews teach about leadership development as a long process that is learned through years of practice; they point to Colin Powell as the ultimate example of exemplary followership.

As the youngest person ever elevated to the position of chairman of the Joint Chiefs of Staff at the age of fifty-two, Colin Powell acted as the senior military counselor to President George W. Bush and to the secretary of defense. Although he rose as a leader, most of his career entailed follower-type positions, including the following key positions: executive assistant to the special assistant to the secretary and the deputy secretary of defense, senior military assistant to the deputy secretary of defense, deputy assistant to the president for national security affairs. Powell exuded the attributes of effective followers: honesty, dependability, competence, courage, enthusiasm, assertiveness, and independent critical judgment.

The common theme found in these military leaders is that none of them were born great leaders; they all spent decades developing their leadership skills. These military leaders were also great followers; as with General Colin Powell, leaders in the military must learn to be great followers before they will be trusted to take on leadership roles; even in the highest rankings as leaders, they are viewed by their superiors as great followers.

Regardless of your career or calling in life, you will be either a follower or a leader. As a leader you will also find yourself in a follower role — as Head of State, you answer to the people and other arms of government. As a CEO, you answer to your board, your leadership team, your customers and your community. As a head of an organization you answer to your customers, your superiors and your leadership team. As a head of a team, you answer to your team and your superiors. We are always leading and following all at the same time. Despite your role, you can choose to lead and follow with integrity, honesty, collaboration, excellent communication, always keeping your values at the forefront. All of these values used concurrently establish trust, and trust is the one thing you absolutely must establish to become an effective values-based leader.

QUESTIONS TO KEEP YOU THINKING

1. What values do you lead (and follow) with?

2. How do your people (or people around you) know your values?

3. How do you permeate those values through your organization?

4. Of the values that Laver and Matthews introduce in *The Art of Command* through historical and contemporary examples, which do you find most effective in getting things done?

Be, Know, Do

C.D.M. Malone states that a definition of leadership in the military does not begin with the definition, but instead, with the mission of military leadership. The central mission of army leadership is driven by these components: *Be, Know, Do*. In other words, regardless of rank or title, BE (who you are inside), KNOW (your bank of knowledge), DO (your actions).

These army leadership principles are particularly relevant to civilian application as they encompass overall growth and personal development toward a singular purpose—achieving one's mission. In their book, *Be-Know-Do: Leadership the*

Army Way, Frances Hesselbein and Eric K. Shinseki outline the leadership philosophy for arguably one of the best-run organizations in the world.

BE

Character happens when you are alone, and that is what BE is all about. With that in mind, who is the leader? What does the leader stand for? Army leadership begins with who the leader is inside and the character of the leader. In order to lead others, the leader must make sure his or her own house is in order. Following are the Army's seven core values; they guide the Army leader and form the acronym LDRSHIP. These seven values exemplify the character of the leader as follows: *Loyalty, Duty, Respect, Selfless service, Honor, Integrity, and Personal courage* ➔ *LDRSHIP.*

In addition to these seven values, Hesselbein and Shinseki suggest mental, physical, and emotional attributes for an Army leader to influence the unit or organization. The *mental* attributes include *Will, Self-discipline, Initiative, Judgment, Self-confidence, Intelligence, and Cultural awareness.* The *physical* attributes include *Health and Physical fitness, and Military and Professional Bearing,* which can be developed. According to the Oxford Dictionary, *bearing* means: "The way one behaves or conducts oneself, an example they give is *"she has the bearing of a First Lady."*

Emotional attributes include *Self-control, Balance, and Stability;* these control how the leader feels; therefore, they play a part in how the leader interacts with his or her subordinates. "When you understand that will and endurance come from emotional energy, you possess a powerful leadership tool." In order to make the right ethical choices, self-control, balance, and stability must be followed.

In addition to understanding the Army values and leader attributes, the Army leader must also embrace and live them, and teach them to their subordinates through action and example. My mother used to say to me as I was growing up: "Actions speak louder than words," therefore, actions are how leaders develop leaders, and by the way, actions are how parents develop their children too.

These core character values and attributes translate seamlessly to the civilian world, as they are highly esteemed in the private sector. Think about it—if every one of your employees operated with the core values of loyalty, duty, respect, selfless service, honor, integrity, and personal courage and lived out those beliefs through actions, your job as a leader would simply be to inspire their actions.

KNOW

The best way to get people to follow is by demonstrating knowledge, hence the KNOW in the Army's mantra. Incompetence is the quickest way for leaders to lose trust and commitment from their followers. According to Hesselbein and Shinseki, a leader must have mastery of the following four skills:

> *Interpersonal skills.* These include coaching, communicating, empowering individuals, and building teams.

Conceptual skills. Critical thinking, analytical skills, and the ability to think creatively and thoughtfully are determinants of ethical sound judgment.

Technical skills. This includes the ability to get the job done. The leader must possess the skills necessary to accomplish the mission.

Tactical skills. This includes problem solving to achieve the objective. In the civilian world, these include negotiation skills, human relations, budgeting, and the like; these are necessary to accomplish the task.

ALWAYS MAKE IT PERSONAL.

US Navy Vice Admiral Raquel C. Bono has utilized all four of the above skills throughout her career as a US Navy command surgeon, both at home and abroad. Once Vice Admiral Bono realized she could be part of the navy leadership and make a difference in the lives of her colleagues and patients, she knew that she had to make changes to her skill set to align her career path to her vision:

> *I realized the only person doctors would listen to was another doctor. I became proficient as a surgeon and was always trying to understand where my colleagues were coming from as well as to unobtrusively help them to be empathetic to patients. I listened to both patients and administrators to initiate real change. That was when I realized I could be more than a surgeon. I began*

*to appreciate being a part of a bigger purpose. I never
stopped learning, and I always made it personal.*

The best leaders are constantly learning; they seek out
opportunities that stretch and challenge them to continuously
become better. They consistently look for mentors—reverse
mentors in some cases—and surround themselves with people
from whom they can learn.

The Army leadership framework makes a distinction between
performing actions and developing skills. It encourages the
military officer to engage in continuous learning, with every
rank being a practice ground for the next assignment, and the
next one, and the next one, and so on. Soldiers are encouraged to
learn more and move to jobs with increasing responsibility, where
they will face new responsibilities, new equipment, new ideas,
and new ways of thinking. These will, in turn, be learned, and
the soldier must learn to apply these skills in accomplishing his
or her mission. *Be* and *Know* represent character and knowledge.
But these two alone are not much without actions. As we all can
agree, *actions speak louder than words.*

DO

Army leaders are known to take their troops to practice their
skills prior to arriving at the combat training center. It's all about
action, or what they DO. They take advantage of every chance to
improve themselves and their people. According to Hesselbein
and Shinseki, successful leaders act in three ways: (a) they pull
their people together and lead them with a common vision and
purpose, (b) they execute flawlessly in order to achieve the desired
results, and (c) they focus on creating a stronger organization

through leading change. That is their legacy. These three actions are called by the Army influencing, operating, and improving.

Influencing. This includes making decisions, communicating those decisions to teams, and motivating and inspiring people toward the desired results. This influencing often happens face-to-face, when the leader coaches followers in the field, gives them praise, and encourages hard work. While higher leaders influence their direct reports through personal contact, they influence their organizations through indirect means. Influence is critical at all levels of the organization.

Operating. Effective leaders execute flawlessly on their plans. They put together detailed, executable plans, then they execute flawlessly those plans while taking care of their people and creating results. Please note that what makes a great leader (as compared to a good one) is the critical distinction of *putting people before results.* More on that later. Once the plans are implemented, they work toward the sustainability of what they have created; ensuring effectiveness and efficiency of their plans. This leads to the third leader action.

Improving. While most leaders focus on short-term wins, effective leaders focus on leaving the organization better than they found it. They take the necessary steps to improve every area they touch, and focus on how they can influence the positive outcome of future missions. Loyal leaders focus on the future of the organization, not just on executing their plan for today. They invest the time and resources to develop themselves in order to be better for their people. They constantly groom and invest in their people by allowing them to learn from their mistakes instead of expecting perfection. They understand that breakdowns are specifically designed to create breakthroughs, and when breakdowns happen, instead of looking for a fall guy, they seek to understand and learn from the break downs in order to create a better organization for the future. This in turn inspires their teams to continue to grow without fear of retaliation for imperfection. This type of behavior is consistent with Kouzes and Posner's findings where honesty is one of the top leadership characteristics people admire in someone they are willingly follow.[29]

Continuous development is part of the culture in military service. Physical, mental, and social skills development are part of every military leader as they condition physically, focus on teamwork, and train for making decisions. Basic values are also taught and continuously reinforced in order to accomplish military missions. Each branch of the military reinforces values from the moment cadets enter training.

The Marine Corps has an ethos of Duty, Honor, Country. The Air Force implements core values of Integrity, Service, and Excellence. The Navy teaches core values in the charter of Honor, Courage, and Commitment. The Army values of

Loyalty, Duty, Respect, Selfless service, Honor, Integrity, and Personal courage, which form the acronym LDRSHIP.

Fostering and developing the leadership values above undoubtedly leads to exemplary results. According to The Congressional Medal of Honor Society, The Medal of Honor is the highest award for valor in action against an enemy force, which can be bestowed upon an individual serving in the Armed Services of the United States. It is the highest awarded by the President of the United States on behalf of Congress. As of this writing, a total of 3,515 recipients received the Medal of Honor; of these, nineteen of them are double recipients.[30] One of the most recent was awarded to Sgt. Dakota L. Meyer for his courage and steadfast devotion to his U.S. and Afghan comrades in the face of almost certain death.

Sgt. Meyer went with two platoons of Afghan national army and border police into the village of Ganjgal for a meeting with village elders. The patrol was ambushed by more than fifty enemy fighters; Sgt. Meyer seized the initiative when he heard over the radio that four of his team members were cut off. Sgt. Meyer returned to the combat zone five times to disrupt the enemy attack and locate the trapped U.S. soldiers. His actions inspired the members of the combined force to fight on.

There is a great deal that can be learned from studying the leadership development techniques of the military, as the armed forces consistently churn out some of the most hard-working, focused men and women who lead with strength and integrity.

QUESTIONS TO KEEP YOU THINKING

1. How do the Army's leadership themes—*Be, Know, Do*—show up in your current role as a leader?

2. In which leadership theme do you find your team most lacking?

3. What can you do as a leader to encourage development of the mission of *Be, Know, Do* in your organization?

4. As you reflect on this chapter so far, what is the one take-away you have realized that you can do to make you and your team better (more effective, efficient, collaborative, trust each other)?

Most Admired Leadership Characteristics

Ideally, we can all name former leaders or mentors who shaped us as followers into the leaders we are today. They likely showed interest in our career, possibly even our personal lives, and made us want to be better, smarter, and *more* than we dreamed for ourselves. Or perhaps you had an inner drive that made you strive to succeed, whatever the cost, and followed other leaders as a means to an end. The question is, what makes a leader someone others want to follow?

In their aforementioned book, *The Leadership Challenge,* Kouzes and Posner surveyed thousands of people in business and government, asking these leaders to cite the leadership characters they admire in their leader. Their definition of leader was someone people would be willing to follow. The key word here was *willing.* The participants would follow these leaders because they want to, not because they have to. To date, Kouzes and Posner have administered their survey to more than 75,000 people around the globe, and their findings are updated continuously. After more than two decades of asking these questions around the world, they found remarkably consistent results. It appears a person must pass several tests before he or she is considered to be a leader. Over time, only four characteristics have received more than 50 percent of the votes consistently. To follow someone willingly, people want leaders who are honest, forward looking, competent, and inspiring.

Honest. Honesty was selected more often than any other characteristic; it emerges as the most important ingredient in the leader-follower relationship. Studies have shown that leadership is getting results in a way that inspires trust, and building trust not only creates followers, but also increases productivity and lowers cost.[5]

Forward looking. More than 70 percent of participants in the Kouzes & Posner study selected the ability to look ahead as one of the most important leadership traits for people they would choose to follow. People expect to have a sense of direction and want to follow someone who has a way of looking ahead and articulating clearly his or her vision. It is important to note that 95 percent of senior executives who participated in the Kouzes & Posner study selected "forward looking" as a desired leadership characteristic, whereas 60 percent of frontline supervisors selected "forward looking" as their top leadership characteristic. This wide gap may indicate a significant difference in expectations, depending on the time in job and the scope of the job; the higher in the organization, the more expectation to look ahead.

Competent. In order for someone to follow a leader, he or she must believe that leader has the competency to guide. Leadership competence refers to a leaders' track record of performance and their ability and confidence to get things done. This does not mean that leaders must have the most practical experience of details around the core technology of their operations. The type of competency demanded appears to vary more with the leader's position and the condition of the organization. Leaders can't be expected to be the best technically competent in their fields; however, they are expected to be competent in taking the organization to a desired future state. This depends entirely on the state of the organization when the leader takes it over, and their ability of the leader to take their organization to a future state.

Inspiring. Leaders are expected to be enthusiastic, energetic, and positive about the future. They are expected to be inspiring by being able to communicate the vision in ways that encourage their teams to sign up for the duration. Inspiring leaders speak to employees' desires to have meaning and purpose in their lives. This is especially critical in times of uncertainty when leading with positive emotions is absolutely important to moving people forward and inspiring them to follow a common vision.

These four traits translate to credibility, which is the foundation of leadership, according to their research. However, what behaviors show credibility? Kouzes and Posner found the following common phrases among people's descriptions of credible leaders:

- ✴ "Leaders practice what they preach."
- ✴ "They walk the talk."
- ✴ "Their actions are consistent with their words."

- "They put their money where their mouth is."

- "They follow through on their promises."

- "They do what they say they will do."

These are consistent with the Army's three components of leadership: Be, Know, and Do, and what has been presented as the military's way to train their leaders. In contrast, the following leadership principles were defined in the 1965 version of Field Manual 22-100, and are still in the foundation of military training:

- Be technically and tactically proficient

- Know yourself and seek self-improvement

- Know your men and look out for their welfare

- Keep your men informed

- Set the example

- Insure that the task is understood, supervised, and accomplished

- Train your men as a team

- Make sound and timely decisions

- Develop a sense of responsibility in accordance with its capabilities

- Seek responsibility and take responsibility for your actions.

These leadership principles add to and enhance, rather than detract from, the corporate principles that distinguish the credible, honest, forward-looking, inspiring, and competent leader that Kouzes and Posner found people are willing to follow.

Though there are some divergences in approach, there is much that the civilian and military sectors have in common when speaking of leadership focus. One of the key underlying assumptions found in both arenas are those of values. At the end of the day, people's values are what drive them. Both corporate and military values are central to the formation and development of organizational culture, and we have already learned that a positive corporate culture is what determines overall performance and creates results.

QUESTIONS TO KEEP YOU THINKING

1. Take a moment to think about the leaders or mentors that have played a part in your career and leadership development. What key characteristics or values made them someone you wanted to follow? Explain.

2. Compare the people's description of credible leaders as discovered by Kouzes & Posner and the leadership principles defined in the 1965 Army Field Manual 22-100.

    a. How are they the same and how does that apply to your current role as a leader?

    b. What specific activities will you do differently as a result of reading this chapter?

CHAPTER SUMMARY – Key Takeaways

1. The United States armed forces place a great emphasis on leadership training for military cadets and officers from all four U.S. service academies.

2. Effective military leaders must possess nine themes or values: integrity, determination, institutional know-how, cross-cultural knowledge, charismatic and visionary

leadership, technological savvy, adaptive leadership, and exemplary followership.

3. The definition of leadership in the military begins with a defined set of values in the Army, Navy, Airforce and Marines; they all focus on leadership development at every level of the organization — the army's central mission is driven by the components *Be, Know, Do.*

4. In order to follow someone willingly, people want leaders with the most admired qualities: honest, forward looking, competence, and inspiring, with honesty being the top quality everyone looks for.

5. Trust and Credibility are the foundation of leadership.

6. There are many similarities between corporate and military leadership and they both have much to learn from one another.

7. Our job as leaders is to inspire others to follow and walk alongside us through collaboration, authentic and transparent communication, which in turn builds trust.

8. Trust creates a synergy that yields sustainable great results and win-wins for everyone. It's that simple. It's all about the people.

Celebrating a happy moment with my firstborn son, Kristopher

Betty with her daughters, Sandra (left) and Alexandria (right)

Learning about the changes that education has made to the girls from Hope, one of the students in Kenya.

In Kenya with friend and donor Sherry Phelan and Wilter (the girl who escaped circumcision and being traded for marriage by escaping and going into the jungle so she could study instead). She is now in college.

With the Massai Warriors before my daily run. Jackson (standing to my left) was my daily running partner. Jonathan (standing to my right) was the walking companion to my friend Sherry and the rest of the group.

Four girls, all of whom were certain they wanted to be a pilot, a judge, a newspaper reporter, and a neurosurgeon.

Hope hugged me after I told her I am raising funds for college scholarships

L.A.Life
Impacting the Lives of Over a Thousand Women at the
"Women Making A Difference Conference"

Overjoyed by the opportunity to make a difference for these kids!

Betty Speaking to Over 500 Executives in San Diego at the
"Inspiring Leaders to Succeed" Event

CEO Harris Simmons, standing by his father's picture, who was the previous CEO before him—a total of three generations of consecutive family CEOs of Zions Bancorporation.

Lt. Gen. Kicklighter and his beautiful wife Betty hosted me at the Pentagon Offices Club while visiting the summer of 2016

Mission accomplished! Broke ground on a new school in Kenya, Africa.

Breaking ground for the new school in Kenya, from left to right: John Phelan, donor; Cynthia Kersey, CEO of the Unstoppable Foundation; Sherry Phelan, donor; Dr. Betty Uribe; Warren Moon, former NFL quarterback

Stephen Covey and Dr. Betty

Growing up in Colombia; from top left, clockwise: Ricardo, Betty, Fernando, Beatriz (mother), Carlos, Luis Carlos (father).

CHAPTER EIGHT

Choosing the Right People

*"People won't care about how much you know until they know
how much you care."*
— John C. Maxwell

People can be complicated, and they can also be extraordinary.
Effective leadership is walking that fine line between encouraging
the best from the people around you and downplaying the
negative. When you are living with and working with people, you
will experience challenges. It's a given.

You have a choice to engage authentically with everyone around
you, seeking to understand and communicate with them rather
than dismissing them as irrelevant. Little things make a difference.
For example, whenever I interview a potential employee, I always
ask the receptionist how the individual treated them while they
were waiting. Why? The way you treat everyone, regardless of title
or importance, ultimately speaks to your values. I want people on
my team who seek to respect and validate every employee, from
the meek to the mighty.

In a leadership role, this could mean communicating openly with your people, getting to know them in an authentic way, and listening to them. In everyday life, this could mean extending a heartfelt greeting to servers in a restaurant, thanking a friend for their time, looking a coworker in the eyes when you speak to them, or offering help when needed. There is no such thing as a neutral touch. Every touch either adds or depletes value.

People who live with values at the core of their being touch everyone around them in an authentic way that resonates long after they leave.

I shared in chapter four that when I began my journey at California Bank and Trust, I met with and talked to over 550 people in the division personally to get to know them and assess their personal goals. We did something similar with customer focus groups in San Francisco, Los Angeles, Orange County and San Diego. The objective? I wanted each individual to know that I cared about them and valued their input. I wanted to *get in the water* with them.

Allow me to explain.

In his book *The One-Minute Manager*, Ken Blanchard shares a story of how a businessman marveled at how the trainers at Sea World were able to get the 5,000-10,000 pound mammals to do what they wanted them to do. What the trainer told him is the basis for the entire book—it's about using positive, rather than negative, reinforcement with the people in your life, whether they are your family or colleagues. Part of that training involves building trust. When asked how the trainers build trust with their animals, they answer: "We get in the water with them because it's important they know that we mean them no harm." This has become a fundamental principal and core value in leadership for me and also for my teams. I never ask my people to do anything that I'm not willing to do myself. I get in the water with them—this means coaching from the field, not from the sidelines; going out into their world and learning about how their world works. You can't possibly be an effective leader if you don't get in the water with your people. This can also be applied in every area of leadership: government, corporate, the military, academia, sports, music, health, you name it! By getting in the water with your people, you build trust, understand what is really happening in your business, and you identify core issues before they get out of hand. People get to know you as a person and build relationship with you.

We can do the same as leaders by figuratively getting in the water with our people, going to where they are and getting to know them on a personal and professional level. It's what makes my turnaround strategy so successful. When people know that you truly care about them, you will inevitably create authentic buy-in and genuine trust.

Even when you lead and live with values and strive to create trust, you will encounter people who are resistant to the vision and goals that you endeavor to attain. The study participants cited problems in three different areas in relation to dealing with people in an organizational setting: adapting to change, alignment with goals, and communication.

Every leader deals with similar issues. These issues are universal in scope, and they can be overcome as a values-based leader.

An Executive VP at a major banking institution admits that some of their employees are challenged with the speed in which they are expected to adapt to a new way of doing things:

> *My strategy is changing because we are one bank with everyone bringing different skill sets. For example, some banks we bought were savings and loans. Two-thirds of my branches were all new. Because we have decreased transactions, we've had to spend time on labor management, sales management, performance management, and compliance. We needed to communicate to our people that, in today's environment, we have to manage at the speed of change. Customers expect faster service, and we are leveraging technology to help us lead in our market. We educate our employees through training on how to deal with millennials, baby boomers, etc. and around goal methodology. I honestly don't have a lot of empathy, but I do understand that getting folks to adapt to a different direction is not like flipping a light switch. Change takes time.*

A major general in the US Army speaks to the challenges of change in the military sector:

> *In the military, leadership changes every two years, so it is up to the leadership to make people understand that the organization has to change and evolve in order to be successful. How do we do that? We get them involved in the process, bringing them along with prioritizing changes, understanding options and how to attack them, and getting them involved in the ownership of*

*the change. Establish agreement on the vision, even with any shortcomings, institute co-development of a short plan, and then **do it together**.*

Retired US Army General Mick Kicklighter asserts that the world is a very new and different place since 9/11:

There are very few people who, in my opinion, understand the risk that we face. The challenge, then, is to make ourselves relevant to the needs of the nation and to develop the skill sets necessary to make a meaningful contribution. We look at critical infrastructure, cyber security, and cyber defense. We're working with a lot of people in that arena and using education to train the right leaders for this world. Despite the challenges of preparing them for the world we're living in, we keep pushing the envelope and asking for new developments, new patents and ideas. I've got some really great young people who are doing work well above their heads because they want to make a contribution. Finding the best and brightest who are committed to a safer America is key to our success overall.

CEO Robert Bard of *Latina Style Magazine* speaks to alignment of goals in a heavily competitive sector with highly intelligent people:

The problem I face is this: my company is a collection of type-A personalities. It is like running a franchise operation where everyone has their own franchise. Everyone owns their own space, but still needs to connect with each other. My challenge is in getting them to work together as a fist instead of five individual fingers. The result is a much bigger impact. Someone needs to be the conductor because I have a lot of incredibly talented violin players.

In his aforementioned work on leadership in times of economic uncertainty, Ram Charan calls for a deep immersion in the operational details of businesses by their leaders. They should take a closer look at the business, not by sitting in the office, but rather by gaining an understanding of what is happening outside the company, understanding customers, and understanding the inside operations of the business. Plans and progress reports are to be revisited daily, and having every leader involved, visible, and in *daily communication* are key. A new guiding principle arises: "hands on, head in."

Again, getting in the water.

Developing Employee Relationships

J. Willard Marriot started off as a young entrepreneur after working his family's sugar beet farm and raising sheep. He learned early on to rely on his own judgment and initiative since he, in his own words, was given the responsibility of a man. His father would tell him what he wanted done, but he would not tell him how to do it: "It was up to me to figure it out by myself." These skills lent themselves well to putting himself through college and to his first franchise business operating an A&W root beer stand. He eventually moved on to the hotel enterprise that now bears his name. He worked tirelessly to grow his business, and he always cared about people. A true hands-on manager, he thoroughly enjoyed the day-to-day operations of the business even after he retired. He loved visiting various Marriot locations and spending time with the ever-growing ranks of hotel associates who—in his eyes—were the secret of his company's success. His conviction that managers should take care of their associates first voiced a deeply held belief that remains the keystone of the company's culture even to this day.[31]

You know that your organization cannot thrive, or even survive, without good, solid, engaged employees. But how do you find these people? What do you look for when interviewing potential leaders?

I asked my study participants that question; they look for confidence, energy, creativity, out-of-the-box thinkers, a strong desire to learn and grow, proactive, courageous, and capable. They also knew what they didn't want, as General Mick Kicklighter asserted:

> *The thing I didn't want was people who were self-serving, egotistical, overambitious, do-anything-to-get-ahead, sacrificing anything to be successful. That's something I would not tolerate. I would give people second chances in most everything, but not when it came to integrity.*

Integrity was mentioned several times during the interviews, but the results were more than just a list of quantifiable qualifiers. What it came down to was that the high-level executives and military commanders and generals were looking for three different types of employee characteristics:

1. Personality/Strengths profile

2. Skill set

3. Values

All three types are equally important, and they will ideally exhibit themselves in a combination of employees that work together to form a successful team. I wanted to go deeper than the average assessment test to discover what top personality characteristics the most successful values-based leaders looked for when adding to their teams.

Maximizing Personalities

CEO and Founder of LAB Holdings (short for Little American Business) Shaheen Sadeghi is as passionate about inspiring his employees as he is about turning "business-as-usual" on its head. He is constantly trying to look at things in a new way, shattering preconceived notions about organizational culture. Because of his diverse creative background that spans several continents and industries, he looks for that same diversity in his team.

> *I'm always looking for that magic ingredient: those people that have the left and right side of their brains working. I'm just as interested in someone's ability to sketch or paint as I am in their proficiency in creating a balance sheet or income statement. Complacency is my biggest fear—we're only as good as our last album, so to speak. We have to reinvent every quarter, so we can't become complacent.*

Sadeghi admits that these types of people are hard to find, but he is encouraged by current employees like his right hand Chris Bennett, Director of Development for his company, who is both adept at balance sheets and a brilliant chalk artist. This interest in the "whole person" goes beyond what an employee can do for you. It speaks to a desire to surround oneself with like-minded people with whom you can grow and innovate in your industry.

I had the opportunity to also interview Shaheen's right hand, Chris Bennett. He mentioned that something he is very proud of, is the leadership's ability to take individuals from all walks of life who are bright and talented, and create an environment where they are valued, trusted, and their voice is heard. He does this by hiring people who have a unique ability (what I call their genius), and matching that unique ability to their job. This is how he is able to maximize individual personalities and unique talents while creating masterpiece projects that make a difference in the community.

Chris and Shaheen are responsible for several community projects where they revitalize entire communities to create "anti-malls" like the Packing House Food Hall in downtown Anaheim, California, where they celebrate and highlight local artisans, creating art galleries, breweries, yoga and coffee shops while preserving the culture and creating community.

Pablo Schneider, CEO of The Wider Net, a firm dedicated to advancing diverse leaders in top executive leadership and corporate board positions, seeks out people based on their story and their world view. He looks for honesty, integrity, kind-heartedness, respect, dignity, all characteristics of a servant leader. Among those more profound qualities, Schneider also seeks out individuals who have expertise in their field, are excellent communicators, and have influence.

I want to know how adept they are at wielding power to achieve objectives, how they handle stewardship of resources, and their place in group dynamics. I'm looking for strong leaders who develop their own style, processes, models, as well as learning from others along the way.

CEO Matt Toledo of the *LA Business Journal* stated that he surrounds himself with people who he believes are intelligent, healthy both mentally and physically, and have a high level of energy. He says of the non-quantifiable qualities:

I can train people to do anything that they're motivated to do, but I can't train someone to have those non-quantifiable characteristics. I can't train someone to be healthy. I can't train someone to have a strong self-concept. I can't train somebody to have a high level of energy. Those leadership qualities are the building blocks or the DNA of good leaders.

Lynn Carter seeks out those who display characteristics of courage:

Courage gets you out of your comfort zone. This was especially crucial during the last decade in our business. It was changing fast because of the external environment but also because of the complexity of the finance industry. That kind of fast pace necessitates those with courage in order to flourish.

Where does courage originate? With a strong sense of self.

Many of the participants listed self-assurance as a desirable trait in their leadership teams. They looked for confidence, someone who was willing to stand up to them (no "yes men or women"), and someone who felt comfortable with a degree of ambiguity, looking at it as an opportunity. Like J.W. Marriot, they are able to "figure it out for themselves."

Several leaders cited self-motivation, discipline, and a strong work ethic as desirable traits, and it's no wonder. You understand as a leader that those who are self-driven and disciplined produce better results with less management involvement. They are gems to be treasured when you discover them. Not surprisingly, General Julie A. Bentz, PhD said she wants a leader who is self-motivated:

> *I want someone who can take an idea and run with it. They are the ones who look me in the eye and say, "Got it! I'll come back." They don't need a fire lit under them—they are self-motivating.*

Self-motivated individuals are often lifelong learners. Many leaders in the study expressed a desire for employees who were well-read and perpetual students, always learning and making themselves better. One leader said he looks for a "strong thirst and desire to learn and grow." That kind of person will always be willing to go the extra mile to learn a new program or procedure, never questioning if it is part of their job description. They will simply delight in the process of gaining more knowledge.

QUESTIONS TO KEEP YOU THINKING

1. Make a short list of the personality traits you look for when interviewing potential employees. How does your list correspond to the study participants' desired qualities? How do they differ?

2. How do you build trust with your current team?

3. What three key takeaways do you have that you will implement in your leadership journey?

Looking for Various Skill Sets

It goes without saying that you need people on your team who have the innate talents and abilities, as well s the diverse training to execute their jobs successfully. These leadership qualities can be both quantitative and qualitative in nature. When asked what leadership and job skills they look for, participants responded with a variety of answers: great track record, excellent communication skills, collaborative mindset, diverse experience, the ability to solve problems, and an aptitude for strategic thinking.

As far as track record, it's the reason resumes are written and evaluated in the interview process. However, you must be careful when reading a resume, as sometimes looks can be deceiving. When looking for "a track record of top performance," being "the best" or "the #1 performer" is relative. I recently had the opportunity to have a quick conversation with someone who wrote on their resume they were "The #1 Performer" in their organization, only to find out that their skillset did not match the skillset that would make someone successful in our organization. You want people on your team who have proven themselves consistently in areas that are critical to your organization, and have a history of success. Retired US Army General Mick Kicklighter says this about track record as it relates to military application:

> *I look for personnel with a track record known either by me or others with proven performance and with the skill sets needed for each individual situation. Preparing to go into combat is a completely different set of skills than someone you want to run for office in the Pentagon, for example. I look for a track record of integrity as well. Either you have it or you don't.*

Former president of Capital One Lynn Carter added that along with a superb track record, she looks for people who have diverse backgrounds: "Diversity of experience can play a large role in how people come together." Coming together in a successful collaborative experience has everything to do with adding team-oriented people to your staff. Those employees bring value to their team, communicate effectively, understand that people work for people, and have a drive to help one another succeed. Lynn Carter goes on to say:

> *I truly value team-oriented personnel. No one can do it on their own, no matter how smart or how good they are in their position. They must respect opposing points of view. This respect is very challenging to demonstrate initially when building a team (getting past the eye rolling, people tuning out). Yet over time if a team works cohesively to build each other up within that structure, the whole team is lifted up.*

The interview participants also looked for skill sets that include strategic thinking. When charged with the successful completion of multiple high-level projects and managing the people who make it happen, it is essential to have someone on point who thinks and acts strategically. They need to first understand their own role then understand how to create an engaged workforce to make things happen. Nothing is certain in life except the fact that there will be changes and turnovers. Your leaders must be constantly thinking about those they can mentor to become leaders. If there are no potential leaders, it might be time to clean house. Former president and chairman of American Airlines Robert Crandall says, *"You put together the best team that you can with the players you've got, and replace those who aren't good enough."*

I would replace that last phrase, "not good enough," to "not willing to develop and grow." Sometimes it is easier to start fresh and train someone who is motivated rather than trying to change someone who is unwilling to take on the challenge. Only you know what you need and desire for your leadership team.

QUESTIONS TO KEEP YOU THINKING

1. Which skill sets do you look for when hiring people?

2. Which ones are most challenging to identify in an interview setting? Explain.

3. Who do you have on your team that is unwilling to do what it takes to do the job?

4. Would you terminate an employee for not showing growth potential or expend the time, energy, and money to develop them further?

Choosing the Right Employees

We cannot finish this chapter without addressing the employee values that executives covet most in prospective and current employees. Predictably, my interview subjects had a lot to say about values since values were at the core of their own leadership philosophies. When asked what they look for in their employees, they mentioned *integrity, caring, ethical, humility, moral courage, honesty, loyalty, trust, responsibility,* and *a sense of belief or faith.* Several also added that it was important for their employees to have good values in general that aligned with their own and their company's core values.

One of the things I have found through the years is to ensure my employees are clear about my personal values and those of my company. When I interview employees, I let them know my values, which are as follows: God, Family, Career, Health, Education, and Community—in that order. I tell them they don't have to have the same values, but it's important that they know mine as I set the tone for the culture of the organization. I proceed to tell them our core company values and how those align with my personal values; this gives me an opportunity to tell them why I chose my employer and how important it is for me to work in an environment that aligns with my own values. I also share my personal story with them so they know that I too have a story, and they see me as a human being—not just the Executive Vice President—which is just a title that can alienate me from my people. Once I tell them my values, I ask them: "What about you? What do YOU value most?" We talk about their family, their upbringing, what brought them to the company, and they relax. I've been told many a time by prospective employees that they have never had an interview like that, where the interviewer takes the time to allow the candidate to get to know them personally. Of course, we go into their competencies and those required by the job, work history, challenges, etc. But I know beyond a shadow of a doubt that I could make a mistake in hiring someone who doesn't have the competency to do the job as I can teach competencies. I can't teach values, ethics and moral conduct. Those are inherent in the person, and it is mission critical to ensure the people that come into the company are aligned with our core values.

Once again, it all comes down to values.

You could have the smartest person with the most impressive resume in front of you, but if you don't get a sense that their values align with yours, run! There is a higher possibility for friction in the future of your organization.

Two of the most frequent responses for employee values were honesty and caring nature. More than 50 percent of the subjects responded that they valued honesty or integrity. CEO Matt Toledo of the *LA Business Journal* said:

> *I want someone who has integrity and is honest and ethical. It's not what you do but how you do it. It's about the process and how people conduct themselves. As Maya Angelou says, "People will forget what you do but they won't forget how you made them feel."*

In regard to caring, many responded that they looked at how their employees treated other people. However they are treating the people along the way is how they will treat our customers and associates. General Mick Kicklighter acknowledged that he sought out those who had a track record of caring for others, honesty, and integrity. In his opinion:

> *Leaders are people who are both ethical and caring in their positions. They should have integrity in everything they do. If I can't trust you, and you're not honest, I don't want you at all.*

Vice Admiral Raquel C. Bono of the US Navy responded that she values accountability and responsibility:

> *If people are willing to own their actions, take responsibility, no excuses, that is what I really value. For example, if there have been infractions, I want them to come face me. If they said, "I did wrong," I was lenient with them. I have an issue when people don't own their own actions. I don't excuse myself from that accountability either. If you see me responding wrong, let me know.*

When asked what quality he valued most in his team, CEO of Zions Bancorporation Harris Simmons said he looks for people who are *trustworthy*. I asked him, "How do you know someone is trustworthy?" His answer? When they are under stress.

> *Often you don't really know someone is trustworthy until you have experiences with them, see them in different lights, and have seen them under stress. That is when their true character is revealed.*

Simmons shared that he has had his fair share of stressful situations throughout his banking career, but he overcame those challenges by "valuing good people, having good legal advice, and just trying to do the right thing." Having those good people on your team—whose values mirror your own and whom you can trust—is invaluable when navigating challenges. Choosing the right people, then, is key to successful leadership in your organization, and you need to know the key personalities, skill sets, and values that matter to you most.

QUESTIONS TO KEEP YOU THINKING

1. Where do values rank in your assessment of potential employees today—is it even a consideration? Why or why not?

2. After reading this segment, which values resonated most with you as a leader?

3. What values do you look for when interviewing potential candidates, and how do you ensure these get vetted in the interview process?

4. What specific actions will you take to make sure you chose the right people for your company?

Gender: Issues or Opportunities?

I am often asked if being a female has given me an advantage or a disadvantage in my leadership journey. I sought to understand how gender played a role in leadership selection. What I found is that there were both perceived advantages and disadvantages to female leaders in the minds of the executives and military personnel I interviewed.

Perceived Advantages of Women in Leadership

The research from the face-to-face interviews regarding the advantages to women in leadership positions, as shared by the participants, revealed women as nurturers who can build teams and have a high motivation to succeed. They are collaborative, good at building consensus, and natural multitaskers, able to wear different hats effectively.

CEO Matt Toledo shares his thoughts on career, success, and relationships in regard to women:

> *It seems to be a lot more complicated for women than men in my judgment. I think women put more pressure on themselves than men do and, as a result, women are often better performers. I think for a lot of women, there's motivation to succeed that's different from men; and when it's pure and managed, I think it's exceedingly effective. I have a high respect for women in the workplace. I think it comes from the influence of my Aunt Lucia, so it's kind of like in my DNA. I don't understand how women do it. A mom gets up in the morning, gets her kids' lunch made, gets the kids off to school, comes to work, puts in a full day, gets home, makes dinner, makes sure homework is done, gets the kids to bed, does it again and again and again, and is charged with the responsibility of being a good mother, a good parent, getting their kids on*

the right path, and being a performer at their job.
They are super human!

Former president of Capital One Bank Lynn Carter asserts that "women are great multi-taskers and can be open to brainstorming many options; women know how to make trade-offs." Major General Angie Salinas of the US Marine Corps also cited time management skills as a colossal advantage to women in leadership:

> *Time management skills in women leaders are a little tighter than the average person because of the many roles and titles a woman must juggle. To me, that's a talent to have so many roles and be as good as they are in their position. What would normally be associated with disadvantages is really an advantage.*

US Navy Vice Admiral Raquel Bono says:

> *The presence of women in leadership is imperative! Whether in the military, corporate America, or in international relations, it's so valuable. I'm committed to standing in the light in regard to women in leadership.*

Chairwoman Maria Salinas shared her history of often being the only woman on a management team in her corporate career. As a woman, she has a unique perspective on the perceived advantages of women in leadership positions.

> *Whether working in corporate America, doing consulting work, or being in the bank here in a board chair capacity, I have learned that women bring a different perspective. We are not men, so we*

think differently. Especially with so few women in the boardroom, that perspective needs to be seen. Sometimes there are things that are discussed and men can go right to "We need to do this." I might be the only voice that says, "I agree, but have you considered this?" Sometimes men can get to the answer because they're ready to go on to the next thing. My experience has been that we need to make sure the management team is on board, the employees understand it, and our external stakeholders understand it. I'm more analytical in my thinking, and that other perspective is so important in a male-only room. They can come to consensus quicker. I will always be the one to slow things down and ask, "Have we thought of X, Y, and Z?"

The male interview subjects responded with a litany of advantages to women in leadership as well. CEO Mike Reynolds shared how women fit into the structure of his organization and how well it works for him:

I've always looked for a woman to become a partner, a senior executive with me, because women's strengths are way beyond men's strengths, even in the business world. Although it's just coming to fruition now, that has been my perception all along. The areas in which I've been the most successful are those where I have been represented by a woman in that particular market. If you look at the trading business, in which I was obviously a very substantial, qualified trader, I was represented in Canada by a woman. I was represented in the Trader's Association by a woman. Pretty much wherever I was and needed a representative, it was always a woman because I realized early on that woman are exceptionally loyal.

CEO Robert Bard of *Latina Style Magazine* talked about the advantages to women in relation to negotiating, team building, decision making, and building leaders:

When we worked with the FBI, they provided us with research regarding women on special teams. It showed that when they put their teams together to follow fugitives or resolve situations, it was always better when a woman was part of the team because women look at things from a different angle, are better at diffusing conflict, are good negotiators, and they always make the team stronger.

Yes, women are nurturers, but this means they will have a good grasp on nurturing leadership. Look at a woman raising a child—it's similar to what you do in corporate America. You mentor them, bring them through the ranks, etc. Women may be more embracing of this concept of building leaders. Men are more cocoons, alone in my army. My experience is that women are better at putting teams together and building consensus.

A woman gets up, takes care of the kids, then she's off to her job responsibilities. I see this is my wife. She can be sicker than hell, not feeling well, but for her, not performing her duties is not an option. I will sometimes feel tired and don't want to go to an event. My wife will say, "We promised to be there; we'll be there." To her, a promise is sacred.

Another example of a woman whom I admire is my editor. She gets really bad migraines, but she would send out the magazine from the grave. I have such incredible confidence in her. Whatever the cost, it will be done.

Robert continued with his thoughts on the challenges for women in corporate culture:

The challenges for women are there because it's a male-dominated environment. For women to break through, they have to not only be exceptional, but they have to prove themselves at every stage; even then, the woman's credentials are always questioned. Until women are in consistent, large numbers in positions of influence, it will continue to be difficult.

Take a look at Madeline Albright. She was the first female secretary of state, and it took a lot of time for people to accept her. Connie Rice was an exceptional secretary of state—she was an amazing force.

Perceived Disadvantages of Women in Leadership

There were some disadvantages raised during the face-to-face interviews, such as the idea that women are perceived as emotional, lacking credibility, and not always taken seriously. Most leaders shared that women often must work harder, smarter, and more consistently to be acknowledged as leaders. Angie Salinas shared the experience of when she was assigned a new role and how she gained credibility as a woman, as introduced in chapter six:

> *As soon as it was announced I was going to be the training general, 99 percent of retirees (all males) said: why are they sending her here, why not send her to Paris Island where there are women? Their comments were strictly based on my gender. The Hispanic community jumped in, so some of the naysayers would say: the only reason she got the position is because she's a woman, and she's Hispanic. Makes it challenging to walk in and say, "I'm here because I'm the best qualified general officer to be here."*

Yet there was a hopeful tone in many of the interview responses. Retired General Mick Kicklighter sums up the big picture:

> *I just have so much respect for the contributions that women are making in all fields. I don't see this as a woman's job or a man's job. I see it as a leader's job.*

I agree with General Kicklighter; leadership has no gender boundaries. We can grow and develop as leaders ourselves as we learn from the perspective of those who have risen through the ranks of the corporate world and the military and have become successful without sacrificing their values. We can build our teams based on the skills, personalities, and values that matter to us. We can commit to becoming difference-makers who look for those we can train and build up to become the next generation of leaders.

I was recently asked the same question during a live interview from another continent. When I really hard, I had to come to the consensus that being a woman has its advantages AND it's disadvantages. I am often the only woman at the boardroom and when we break, all the men head in the same direction while I head a different direction by myself. One day I was in Utah with our Chairman of the Board and our CEO to meet with a Congresswoman. During a break I asked the Congresswoman: Would you care to use the restroom? As I walked her to the restroom I realized I had her all to myself. We talked some business and solved some issues and there was no one else but just the two of us! Being a woman does have its advantages!

In contrast, I was speaking in Hong Kong to a group of entrepreneurs and top executives. I was being introduced as an entrepreneur and an executive in banking in the United States, and someone who knows how to create win-wins in negotiations. There were only men in the audience—it was a relatively small group of under 100 very successful entrepreneurs—and just as I took the microphone, a man stood up. I hadn't even said one word and he already had a question! He proceeded to ask me about how I could help him create a win-win with his competition when all he wanted to do was crush them; the question was designed to put me in check. I gracefully responded with: "If you would kindly listen to my lecture, you will find the answer during this chat." I had to be respectful of the culture while ensuring my spot as a subject-matter expert. I was asked to speak in Japan and then asked to come back to help empower women in a country where women are not embraced as leaders yet.

When I think of the third world countries I have visited and the role of women, I think of the United States many years ago. Yes, women have come a long way; we can now vote, hold high positions and hold seats at the table. But so have the Asians come a long way in our history, as well as the African Americans, Hispanics, and others. When I think of advantages and disadvantages, I think we all have those: men, women, tall people, short people, heavy, think, brown, black, white, male and female. I think the larger question is this: What are we going to do with what we have?

I was sitting at an intimate dinner with President Bush, Sr. when he stood up and said something about our country that I eventually adapted as my own when it comes to my life journey; he said: "It's not what we have, but what we do with what we have that makes the difference." So I say to you: What will you do with what YOU have? I say to myself every day: What will I do with the gifts I have been entrusted with? So I chose to focus on this, rather than focusing on what disadvantages I may have for being 5'3" tall, thin, Hispanic and Italian, and a woman.

We must learn to live and work with people handling the challenges and problems that arise with our values intact. It's a matter of choosing to engage authentically with everyone around us, seeking to understand and communicate, and recognizing that it's the little things that make a difference.

That is the job of a values-based leader.

QUESTIONS TO KEEP YOU THINKING

1. How can you do a better job of identifying and encouraging your people's natural strengths in order to grow your male and female leaders?

2. What specific actions did you learn from the examples given in this section that you plan to implement in your own world? Make a list.

3. What specific actions will you take to implement these new tactics in your organization?

4. a. When leading your own organization, department or world, what challenges do you face most?

   b. What unique talents or values do you bring to the table that support you in overcoming these challenges?

   c. How do you use these talents or values to grow your subordinates and leaders around you to do the same?

CHAPTER SUMMARY – Key Takeaways

* Values-based leaders select people based on values, purpose and leadership style that align with their own and their organization's value system.

* What leaders want: honesty, confidence, energy, creativity, out-of-the-box thinkers, a strong desire to learn and grow, proactive, courageous, selfless, and capable.

* What they don't want: self-serving, egotistical, overambitious, do-anything-to-get-ahead, sacrificing anything to be successful.

* There are both perceived advantages and disadvantages to women in leadership roles.

* It is the leader's job to identify and encourage the natural strengths and skills sets that their team bring to the table.

* There is no such thing as a neutral touch. Every touch either adds or depletes value. It's up to us which we chose to do.

* It's not what we have, but what we do with what we have that makes the difference.

CHAPTER NINE

Making Decisions

Your decision-making style and process is a
highly accurate barometer of your values.

"It's not hard to make decisions when you know
what your values are."
—Roy E. Disney

This section of the book is titled "Putting It All Together With Values" because internal and external value indicators should naturally follow through to your actions. Putting it all together is essential to living and leading with values. It won't do you any good to know what your values are if you don't know how to incorporate them into your life. Even more importantly, it won't do anyone else any good and will lessen your influence if you don't integrate your values with every action, every decision.

As I often say, "It is not just *what* we have; it is what we *do* with what we have that makes the difference."

What are you doing with your values? Do they just hang on the wall, lettered and displayed as a quaint saying, or are they *etched in your heart* and influencing every decision you make? Decisions are at the very intersection of our values, whether they are big or small. They are of even greater significance when viewed on the grander scale of the corporate, financial, and military settings of the high-profile leaders in this book.

Decision-making is indeed complex and multi-faceted in many instances, but it really is simple when you see it through the lens of your core values. Though Disney's statement above may seem to oversimplify the process of making decisions in a highly complex corporate, military or government environment where leaders face significant and potentially life-changing decisions, the heart of his statement rings true. When you navigate from a place of values, the process of decision-making becomes more straightforward. This is what I call "congruency," where your actions are aligned with your espoused values. It is highly important since leader's decisions from all walks of life could potentially impact hundreds or thousands of people. It is imperative that their decision-making strategy is sound. Just as a leader's character, values and purpose form the foundation for their leadership, their decision-making strategy would ideally demonstrate the implementation of those values.

This is where *intellectual honesty*—a term coined earlier in the book by Harris Simmons—comes in. Intellectual honesty is our ability to be honest with ourselves without rationalizing decisions. It means being willing to tell the truth, even when it is inconvenient. This term is one I'm going to quote for the rest of my life, because it is just that vital to values-based leadership.

Earlier in the book, I touched on the vacuum of values that has permeated every aspect of our culture: business, sports, government, entertainment and even family life. That vacuum originated and began to grow exponentially when people made decision upon decision that did not resonate with their values. They chose a quick thrill, an easy buck, a shortcut rather than hard work, patience, and integrity. I saw enough of the greedy, short-term decision-making that characterized the financial services industry in times of financial stress in the early 2000s. Those decisions showed a lack of values-centered leadership, and I knew there was a better way to lead.

CEO Bob Carr spoke to the determination he has to make decisions from a place of conviction and strength:

> We all have to make tough decisions. We're put in bad circumstances, sometimes of our own making, and we have to have the inner strength to say, "Stop. This is not going to continue. We're going to fix this right now. Ever since I have embraced that inner strength, I've made decisions based on my values, and it's paid off extremely well.

When asked about decision-making in the interviews, every values-based leader I spoke to talked about a specific process they used to make decisions. They utilized risk management, causal analysis, an understanding of the critical factors and economic conditions, as well as collaborative evaluation to define the problem at hand and move forward with decisive action.

As I analyzed the data and reviewed the participant interviews, I sought to find a pattern in the research. It wasn't until a long weekend away in a hotel, where I sequestered myself in order to finish my doctoral dissertation, that the answer was finally revealed.

I had been working with ferocity to complete my dissertation, but the tolls of a full-time job and the responsibilities of my dear children were beginning to wear on me. Waking every day at four in the morning to write before work and staying up well past midnight had left me depleted and discouraged. I was running on fumes but determined to meet my goal of finishing my entire doctorate in three years—which brought me to a quiet hotel room that fateful weekend. My husband wanted to join me as I suggested that I might get more done if not distracted by other obligations, and I gratefully accepted. I set up my computer, research materials covering every surface of the hotel desk, and I began to work. It was extremely overwhelming with the sheer volume of material to analyze, but I forged ahead, seeking to understand what was different about how these leaders made decisions.

All of a sudden, I started to see a pattern. I remembered the words of Angie Salinas, and it all fell into place. There have been few times in my life where I felt like I had a revelation, but this was one of them. Tears came to my eyes as I furiously wrote down notes expounding upon the decision model that was revealing itself through the collective interviews.

It was a strategic, collaborative decision model that incorporated high-potential leaders, along with key stakeholders, in the decision-making process to allow them to learn experientially how decisions are made at a strategic level, while the executive leaders remained cognizant of their own responsibility and ability to be the ultimate decision maker.

The Strategic Collaborative Decision Model was born.

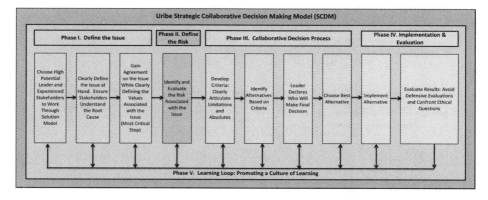

Figure 9-1: Uribe Strategic Collaborative Decision Model

I knew from my research into Peter M. Senge's approach, that a leader should create an environment where people continually expand their capacity to create results, where new and expansive patterns of thinking are nurtured, and where people continually learn how to learn together.[32] The Strategic Collaborative Decision Model summarizes a decision model where less experienced high-potential leaders are purposefully selected to learn from experienced leaders about collaborative decision-making. This Strategic Collaborative Decision Model addresses complex strategic decisions and is organized into five phases:

* *Phase I: Defining the Issue*

* *Phase II: Evaluating the Risks*

* *Phase III: Collaborative Decision Process*

* *Phase IV: Evaluate Results*

* *Phase V: Learning Loop, Promoting a Culture of Learning*

Please note that this decision model is intended for strategic decisions at any level: in government, , in the boardroom, at the executive level, at the management level and even in a family unit. The same principles apply in each situation.

Phase I: Defining the Issue

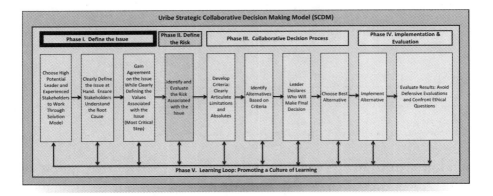

Figure 9-2: Strategic Collaborative Decision Model - Define the Issue

1. **Choose a High Potential Leader.** This phase begins with the top leader choosing the stakeholders who will work through the decision-making process, as well as a high potential leader, whose developmental opportunities lie in the subject at hand.

Stakeholders' Role: These are individuals who have a vested interest in the outcome of the decision, who can bring forth diverse points of view to issues and can most deliberately influence the outcomes of the decision. By including stakeholders, the leader also gains consensus from other leaders, facilitating the buy-in process while making the final decision.

NOTE: Choosing Stakeholders is key in the decision process, and these individuals will vary depending on the type of decisions you will be making. For example, in the last organizational transformation I executed, I was in the process of making choices in the organizational structure of the bank, so I chose stakeholders from every department of the bank: HR, Finance, Marketing, Credit, Legal and Field Operations.

Major General Angie Salinas included a high potential leader as part of her decision process; this allowed her to strengthen her bench strength by growing emerging leaders on-the-job, causing them to actually experience what it's like to be "in her shoes." This continuously reinforces to the high potential leader that they are valued, and also that their voice is heard. This also helps with retention and employee morale, with other potential leaders wanting to get the opportunity to "sit at the table." Stakeholders must clearly define the issues and understand the root causes so they don't accidentally solve for symptoms rather than the real issue.

2. **Clearly Define the Issue**. It is critical that the issue be clear to all stakeholders, as lack of clarity of the issue being addressed could lead to misalignment of the ultimate decision.[33]

Two-star General Julie Bentz, PhD Director for Nuclear Defense Policy, has navigated countless issues and made thousands of decisions, most recently starting a national program with the Department of Homeland Security, to support the U.S. Government. She talks about defining the issue in decision-making:

> *Everyone must realize something is needed, a gap exists. This is when you can begin to build a common vision and get folks on board. You just do what seems impossible to others by taking things step by step and documenting everything.*

Sometimes defining the issue can be problematic if you or your team cannot identify the real issue. Former President of Capital One Lynn Carter says it is crucial to understand what is *really* the problem, as sometimes what you think is the problem is not the real issue. A major general in the US Army adds that sometimes the heat of the moment, especially in regard to military decisions, requires time sensitivity and situational evaluation:

> *Obviously, each situation is different, and the priority you place on any given problem depends on the severity of the situation. Most of the time people are not clear on either the process or the actual problem. The timeline is important, and you often have to pursue multiple options as you analyze and quickly assess throughout each action step.*

CEO Robert Bard of *Latina Style Magazine* offers a perspective from an industry that must deal with a variety of external problems, including community problems:

> *Because of the nature of our business, we get people upset. A leader may see someone was profiled in our magazine while they were not, or people don't like how we cover military issues because they feel we're encouraging their students to join the military. It's every day. First, I have to see the overview of what is happening and define the problem—is it internal, operational, or external? Then I act based on priority. It's a balancing act, and I have to take the bullets all the time.*

When you are a values-based leader, you give priority to the issues that are at the core of your value system. For example, CEO Matt Toledo of the LA Business Journal says this of making decisions with values in mind:

> *I'm pretty straightforward. I run a newspaper, so there are three things I care about—value to the reader, value to my marketing partners, and making money, all in that order. The things I'm faced with on a day-to-day basis revolve around what we're doing as an enterprise. I created the guiding principle of the "three things" years ago because it made it real easy to decide on anything: 1) Does it make sense for the reader? 2) Does it make sense for the market partners? Is it profitable? 3) Is it profitable? If it's all three, great. But if it makes money and doesn't have reader value, I'm probably not going to do it. I look for three out of three in everything I do.*

Defining the issue may seem like an obvious first step, but you would be surprised how many people don't properly address this phase.

3. **Gain Agreement on the Issue**. When defining the issue, it could be helpful to remind all stakeholders of the values that are to be upheld during this particular decision process. In order to avoid an ethical trap, where decision makers fail to understand values that are motivating the questions, all stakeholders must consider company and personal values associated with the issue. Once you reach agreement, you are ready to evaluate the risks.

QUESTION TO KEEP YOU THINKING

1. When making critical decisions about your company, how do you and your team go about "defining the issue at hand" in your organization? Is it more situational, like Lynn Carter and General Kicklighter suggested, or does it depend on values alone?

2. If you had to narrow down your guiding principles to three things as Matt Toledo has (reader value, market partner value, monetary value), what would those three principles be for your organization? Explain.

Phase II: Defining the Risk(s)

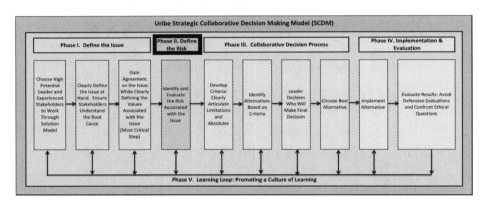

Figure 9-3: Strategic Collaborative Decision Model - Define the Risk

All decisions have a relative risk. For example, spending a large amount of capital to purchase a new company presents a different risk than deciding to move the headquarters from Minnesota to San Francisco. Moving across country for a new job has a myriad of risks. Even deciding whether you should dive into a new relationship is risky. Leaders are required to mitigate a certain amount of risk on a daily basis when making decisions, so the second phase of my decision model requires evaluating risk.

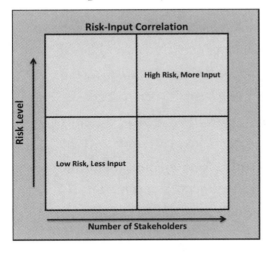

Figure 9-5: Risk-Input Correlation: Risk levels determine quality and quantity of leaders assigned to the decision-making process.

As seen in Figure 9-5, the higher the risk, the more thoughtful the decision process, and the higher consideration for the right stakeholders to bring into the decision process. The level of risk also determines which high potential leader should be assigned to the decision process based on experience, leadership strengths, and learning path. In this model, executives bring a high potential leader to the table so they gain experience from several complex decisions; once they are promoted into C-level positions, they will be able to draw upon their personal experience and the connections they made along the way with more experienced leaders.

Risk may be associated with reputation, brand, financial outcomes, morale of personnel, operational risk, distribution risk, political risk and other risk associated with the potential outcomes of the decision. Once the risk is determined and evaluated, the decision-making process begins. Executive Vice President of a large financial services organization says this of risk:

> *It's all about risk management, not zero risk. You must understand the balance of risk vs. reward based on the analytical process, financial statistics, and supporting documents and views. There are always indirect benefits or takeaways in the form of customer experience, employee experience, corporate culture, or belief system segments. Yet it all starts with the economics and risk management. You cannot avoid risk. You must manage it.*

Earlier in the book I cited Chairwoman Maria Salinas of ProAmerica Bank, who talked about how important excellent communication is in creating buy-in and alignment. She concedes that not everyone will agree, but they must align. She also spoke to her process, which inevitably involves risk assessment.

> *We created a product that we wanted to use with suppliers of major corporations. So when that came through, we had to go through the process of analyzing at the management level, understanding risk, and walking through the how-tos. It was something new for the bank and there was some risk associated with it. We needed to assess it and understand it. At the board level, we sought to understand how the new product fit in with the bigger strategic plan of loan production and the marketing component. We also needed to know the risk outside of just financial risk, such as reputation. Putting that process in place, we identified potential*

issues, researched them, made a recommendation, and made a decision.

Depending on what the decision is, there's got to be a process around it. This is especially true for a bank, where from a regulatory perspective they want to see process: "What were you thinking when you made this decision?" It's one of the most important things that we need to make sure that we're clear on from a banking perspective, because I'm always thinking, "Who's going to second guess this?"

Notice how Maria made sure the issue was clear to all stakeholders involved; she used an agreed-upon process to avoid lack of clarity or misalignment of the ultimate decision. She made sure her process was sound, particularly since the process was subject to review.

In a more personal decision, you can still utilize the evaluation phase to consider your options. In the example of moving across country, for instance, you would weigh the cost of living, the availability of educational resources for your kids, the effect of climate on your energy bills, and the accessibility of public transportation, among many other considerations. In the same way, when faced with the opportunity for a new relationship, you would evaluate risks associated with your emotional health: stability of prospective partner's employment, their physical health, emotional well-being, and health of prior relationships. The most important piece to this phase is honest evaluation. You cannot make a thoughtful decision without first weighing and assessing the risks involved.

Phase III: Collaborative Decision Process

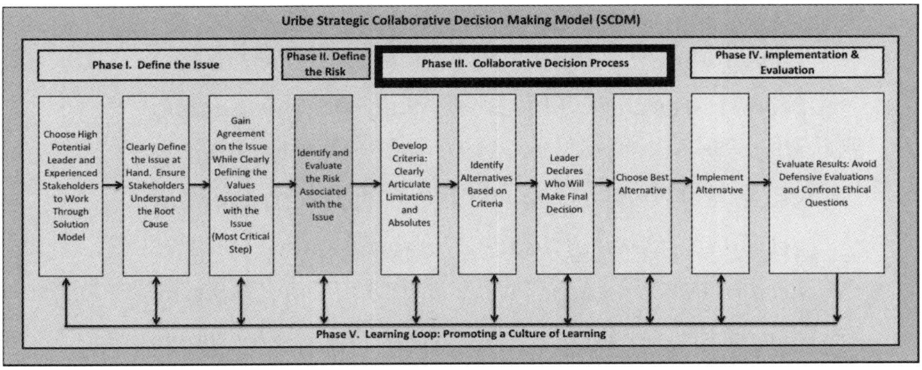

Figure 9-4: Strategic Collaborative Decision Model - Making the Decision

1. **Develop Criteria**. What criteria or values will be utilized to make the decision? This phase begins with taking a critical look at the limitations and absolutes of the situation. Using the business analogy of purchasing another company, limitations may encompass the type of industry the company is engaged in and the geographical locations of their distribution network, where absolutes may include the dollar per share the potential buyer is willing to pay for the company. One of the main values that would be used to make the decision would be cultural alignment—does the corporate culture align with the culture of the purchasing company?

In a more personal example, we could look at how parents handle communicating with their children about an impending divorce. What criteria do they use? 1) They let the children know it's not their fault. 2) The children don't see it as a takeaway (or minimized risk). 3) The children understand that this is the best way to handle the situation. 4) The children feel that they have a voice and are understood. Most couples who go through a divorce don't go through a process like this. They decide to tell the children and, when questions arise, they are unprepared.

2. **Identify Alternative Solutions**. Once the context of the solution is set, alternative solutions are vetted against the limitations and constraints, and *what, where, why, when and how* scenarios, depending on the complexity of the decision.

CEO Mike Reynolds speaks to the idea of his term, "intellectual pooling," in respect to engaging others on his team or advisory board in decision-making:

> *The intellectual pooling philosophy is initially assigned to both the corporate board and advisory board, but what is key for me is intellectual pooling across every level of the company. Everyone participates in this sort of round table discussions where we test particular issues. The purpose is to discuss things that have happened, are going to happen, and where we're going as a company and our overall mission. It's all about relationship building and creating an environment where someone's opinion matters.*

In this open environment, there is a much better chance that there will be abundant, outside-the-box alternatives to the problems presented. This is the type of environment that founder and CEO Shaheen Sadeghi of LAB Holdings strives to maintain with his leadership team, and it comes from his time as a surfer, believe it or not. As a person who loves to inspire people and get his team to think outside the box, he told me that when making a decision, *you can't get a non-surfer to design surfing clothes.* In other words, you need to get into the minds of the people for whom you are making a decision. When Sadeghi makes a decision about what products to promote or what design to champion, he tries to get into the mind of the end user.

> *I want to tap into their souls and learn what they're feeling right now. Focus groups—do you like Coke or Pepsi better—don't do anything. You need to understand what people want and create it from a place of authenticity. That comes from allowing people to be a part of the decision process and removing those layers of management that stifle creativity.*

Both CEOs utilize consensus to make decisions in their businesses, and they do it successfully from a perspective of building relationship, honoring authenticity, and encouraging creative thinking. The key to finding consensus in decision making is in seeking alignment rather than agreement. Alignment has everything to do with values. That's why alignment is required in a military setting. Retired US Army General Mick Kicklighter shared an interesting perspective on decision-making as it relates to the fast-paced problem solving required in combat:

> *In combat, you're watching the situation as it moves rapidly. You have to constantly stay on top of it. As a commander, you can't do that, but your staff can. For instance, you have an operation center, and they're constantly watching the movement of what's happening on the battlefield, and they continually keep you updated. You do analysis, they give you options and possible courses of action, and you*

have to make a choice. What are the consequences of those actions? Sometimes in the military your choices involve the loss of life. You've got to consider the risk, the mission, the possible outcomes, the enemy, but it all happens in mere minutes in the heat of combat.

Even in a mission-critical situation, a leader must have all of the possible alternatives made available in order to make an informed decision.

3. **Leader declares who will make the final decision**. Research shows that collaboration brings forth better decisions. In this model, once clear alternatives are delineated, the leader decides who will make the final decision. It may be that the decision is made based on the group consensus; or if one of the stakeholders has the most to gain or to lose from the final decision, they may be called upon to make the final decision. Depending on the complexity of the issue, the leader holds the responsibility to make the final decision.

US Navy Vice Admiral Raquel Bono speaks to her preference for a collaborative, coaching decision-making process:

I never make the decision. I just articulate the choices, have others articulate what we should do, and get to the point where we are able to endorse it. If I feel something has been overlooked, it's my job to bring it up.

Julie Bentz, Ph.D. Director for Nuclear Defense Policy holds a very high position of authority yet admits to being a "consensus kind of person" in a group setting:

My secret is that I go in early to develop and share a vision. In order to get my people to capture the vision, I put forth questions to articulate purpose and need. Then I articulate the same to the community until there is a shared vision.

Regardless of the process and ultimately depending on the complexity of the issue, the leader holds the responsibility to make the final decision.

4. **Choose best alternative**. Once the decision criteria is set, the best possible solution is made and the team enters Phase IV of the decision model, evaluating results.

Phase IV: Implementing & Evaluating Results

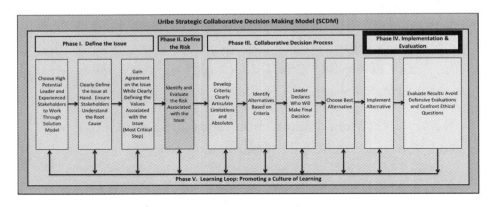

Figure 9-5: Strategic Collaborative Decision Model - Implementation & Evaluation

Once the solution has been implemented, the results are reviewed objectively and quantitatively to determine the effectiveness of the decision. Ethical questions are addressed by clearly understanding the values that are motivating the questions. If the results are as expected, the decision was sound.

If, however, the results did not meet expectations or results exceeded expectations, the team must learn what caused the positive or negative gap as they enter Phase V, the learning loop, promoting a culture of learning.

Retired US Army General Mick Kicklighter already shared how he is known as the "bad news guy," as he encourages hearing the bad news right away in order to deal with it and move on. He is also a strong believer in not dragging out the process:

> There are many forces out there that you need to contend with—some things can go from tactical to strategic catastrophe in a nanosecond on the battlefield. When you've got to deal with a bad situation, you have to do the right amount of due diligence, then you have to make the decision and move to the future and not drag that bag with you.

In other words, you just have to deal with it, evaluate it, learn from it, and move on.

Like Peter Senge, I have always championed the philosophy of creating a learning organization, where members of the team are inspired to learn from each other and where breakdowns are viewed as opportunities to create breakthroughs. This learning environment avoids defensive evaluations, where errors are justified through the learning loop process, rather than used as opportunities for a breakthrough and information researched to support an idea. I learned long ago that creating a safe environment where people are free to "share the bad news," is critical to building trust in an organization and in our families. I remember when my children were little; I taught them that it was okay to make a mistake as long as they didn't lie about it. It was also okay to break things as long as they didn't break them on purpose.

One day we were hosting a party with over thirty people; one of us was carrying a large glass container while walking through the small dining room. The house was full of people and you could hear the music playing and laughter as people shared around the house. All of a sudden the glass container slipped and landed on the marble floor. You can imagine the noise it made, and immediately the buzz stopped. The girls and I broke into celebration and started clapping and saying: "Yay!!!" People looked at us with a puzzled look on their face. People quickly joined in the celebration by seeing us celebrating life and not making it about "who broke the glass container," but instead making it about "isn't it wonderful that everyone is okay." I have brought this to my professional life; I have a large white board in my office, and at the top of the board, I wrote the words: "We Don't do Brain Surgery." Now, for those of you who do, please don't take offense; what I explain to people is, it's okay to make a mistake as long as we are willing to learn from them. Breakdowns are specifically designed to create breakthroughs, if we let them. It's up to us as leaders to create the kind of environment where everyone around us feels valued, respected, and their voice is heard.

Phase V: Learning Loop - Promoting a Culture of Learning

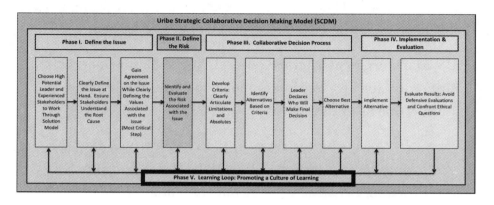

Figure 9-6: Strategic Collaborative Decision Model - Learning Loop

Once outcomes begin to appear, a learning loop is created to ensure stakeholders learn from each phase of the model what worked, what didn't work, and what can be learned that can be applied in the future. A 1974 article by Ian I. Mitroff and Tom R. Featheringham in *Behavioral Science* analyzed systemic problem solving.[34] Borrowing from statistics, alpha (Type I) errors are those that arise when the team rejects a true hypothesis, and beta (Type II) errors arise when the team fails to reject a false hypothesis. A possible example in history was when it was determined that Iraq was an eminent threat based on weapons of mass destruction, although the evidence was not sufficient to make such a statement; this was further reinforced with our failure to bring the troops back. Type III errors are made when a solution solves perfectly the wrong problem; this happens when the problem has been misdiagnosed, or missed altogether during the diagnosis. Again, this is why the phase of Defining the Issue is so important. A typical type III error in medicine, for example, is when the wrong limb is amputated or the money is wired to the right account (according to the form), which happens to belong to the ex-spouse. I know, extreme examples but true life examples that happened when the wrong problem was addressed.

US Marine Corps Major General Angie Salinas served as inspiration for my decision model, and she aptly describes the journey one takes through the process:

> It depends on the severity and complexity of the problem and the issue at hand. If it's a very junior person, I get them to solve the problem but I would ask the questions and encourage them to talk to others, so they collectively get the wisdom from their team. If ramifications are broad, getting senior people and keeping that person involved is important so they can learn. If the problem appears to be the tip of an iceberg, in other words, a bigger issue, then I sit with my leadership team, generate alternative solutions, understand the criteria that need to be evident in the solution, and focus on what's important—Cost? Time? Experience?—then dialogue. It's important to have inclusive conversations with my team about sticky issues; sometimes you can get consensus, but at the end it's important that everyone knows that I am the final decision maker.

Notice how General Salinas recognizes the benefits of collective wisdom, yet she retains the autonomy of the final decision. The best decisions are made when the group leader interacts with group members, focuses on the decision-making process, and increases their team's support and group collaboration, team confidence and quality decision making, which ultimately results in better decisions. This is where the Strategic Collaborative Decision Model shines. Following this model ensures organizations collaboratively solve issues, understanding root causes, reinforcing core values, developing bench strength, and sustaining learning organizations, while avoiding type I, II, and III errors.

CEO of Zions Bancorporation shared in his interview that as a very young president of the company, led by his father, he wanted to make decisions that were the right ones for the right reasons, but he felt paralyzed by what others were thinking. A story from his childhood reinforced his conviction and helped him make tough decisions from a place of confidence:

> *I grew up on an old Arabian horse farm. My dad was out watching me one day as I struggled to put a bridle on the horse. As I tried to slip to bring him back to the barn to get a saddle in order to go horseback riding. As I tried to slip the bridle over the horse's head, standing there facing the horse, the horse was balking. He was not going to move. My dad, who'd been watching the whole time, said, "The horse isn't going to move until you turn around and loosen up, grab the rope, and walk to the barn. Forget you've got a horse behind you and head for the barn." So I did. I turned around, and all of a sudden, the horse followed me. It became a metaphor for my style of leadership and decision-making. I could be worried about what everyone else was thinking, or I could turn around and get things done. I was determined I was going to try to do the right things for the right reasons and appreciate*

the people who were working in this company... and never look back, if you will. I think that was really important in developing the confidence that I could do this and succeed.

The more you practice the different phases of the decision model, the more fluent you will become in the execution of each phase and the more confident you will become in your leadership strengths. Whether you are a strong collaborator or more independent in your decision-making, the process works.

One of the best perks of being a values-based leader is that you are privy to the wisdom of so many amazing leaders who have come before you. If you are already mentoring others or being mentored yourself, I encourage you to include your mentors and mentees in the decision-making process. Look for people who are doing things the right way and follow their lead. CEO Matt Toledo of the LA Business Journal talked to me about how he felt blessed to have great mentors who still influenced him in his everyday decisions:

> *My mentors didn't talk to me or lecture me about doing the right thing. They just did the right thing. So when I'm faced with a difficult decision, I hear their voices in my head. I'm guided by the words and right conduct of the people that I've had the privilege of working with. Those are the voices that guide me when the tough decisions come, as they always do.*

Effective, values-based decision-making doesn't have to be hard when you lead with your values at the core of your reasoning. It may not happen overnight, but when you begin to introduce this decision model and follow it through, you will undoubtedly see change, especially when you practice intellectual honesty.

Nelson Mandela once said, "May your choices reflect your hopes, not your fears." The choices made in the financial downturn were driven by fear and greed. We have a responsibility to choose *better* and *wiser* in order to initiate, facilitate, and nurture real change. It starts with the small decisions and grows exponentially with the big ones. Let your decisions, both big and small, be saturated with your core values, and you will never taste the bitterness of regret.

QUESTIONS TO KEEP YOU THINKING

1. What process do you currently follow when making tough decisions? Explain.

2. How is your decision-making process similar to the collaborative model introduced in this chapter? How does it differ?

3. What key steps will you implement in your decision model to increase the quality of your decisions?

CHAPTER SUMMARY – Key Takeaways

* Your external actions are an accurate indicator of your internal values.

* Every leader has a process for making decisions.

* Values-based leaders make decisions based on their core values.

* The Strategic Collaborative Decision Model has five phases:

- *Phase I: Defining the Issue – avoiding Type III errors*

- *Phase II: Evaluating the Risks – Aligning the decision with core values*

- *Phase III: Collaborative Decision Process – Bringing mentees or high potential leaders into the process*

- *Phase IV: Evaluate Results*

- *Phase V: Learning Loop, Promoting a Culture of Learning – Creating and sustaining a learning organization*

- This decision model focuses on identifying high-potential leaders, along with key stakeholders, who can come alongside current leaders in the decision process to allow them to learn experientially how decisions are made at that level.

- The executive leader still retains the ability to be the ultimate decision maker.

CHAPTER TEN

Dr. Betty's Top Ten Guiding Principles: Advice for the Journey

Many receive advice. Only the wise profit from it.
—Harper Lee

I have had the pleasure of speaking with successful CEOs, titans in the financial industry, high-ranking military leaders, and individuals who lead from the White House and the Pentagon in Washington, D.C. These individuals have had impressive careers and have not wavered from their core values. When I think of someone who is qualified to give advice, these are the people who come to mind. I have soaked up every bit of wisdom possible from each one of them, and I'd like to now share some of that wisdom with you in this chapter.

I have had the honor of speaking to various groups across the country and internationally regarding topics such as leadership, values, courage, taking a stand, respecting one-self, parenting and business turnarounds, to name a few. When I speak to business leaders, I often share my own advice, something I like to call "Dr. Betty's Top Ten." These top ten principles are those that I've gleaned from years of leading my life and directing my career with values as the foundation. It should go without saying that I strive to follow these principles every day of my life, and they are near and dear to my heart. My hope is that you will read these life principles and incorporate some or all of them into your own "top ten" as you navigate your life and leadership journey by these guiding principles:

#1 Lead With Values

This one is obvious, but it bears repeating. As leaders, we need to take tangible steps toward becoming people who put actions to our values. The first step is *knowing* your values, and the second is *following* them without exception. This concept is easy to discuss, yet it's exceptionally challenging to execute, especially in difficult real-life circumstances. However, your values are the only thing worth preserving in the end. Those terminal values of family, health, spirituality, wisdom, and freedom that I talked about in chapter one do not come to those who are short-sighted and without integrity. As I said before, they are the hard-fought rewards of those who both live and lead with values. Former president of Capital One Bank Lynn Carter says it this way:

> *Be true to yourself and your values. Honor what makes you passionate and excited every day. When you do, you will never put yourself in a position that makes you less productive. Stay tied to your values and gravitate toward environments that allow them to be evident, on display. That kind of atmosphere is fulfilling and energizing.*

You will be your best, most authentic self when you honor your values. No, it will not be easy. It was not easy when I restored my father's name by taking on his company's debt in my own name, shaking hands with every creditor face to face, and eventually paying back every penny. It was not easy when I graciously confronted the superior who disrespected me and took the time to dig deeper and understand his motives. It was not easy when I navigated a very difficult hostile takeover, keeping my values in check. I never said it would be easy, but it is most certainly right. As a leader, your people will know you by your actions, and everything flows down from the top. Never underestimate the power of leading with your values.

#2 Protect Your Brand

My brand is featured in the signature line of every e-mail I send out: *Building Trust and Value in Relationships for Generations.* My team and I created that brand to honor our central values, which directly align with my personal values: *building trust* and understanding the *value in relationships,* leaving a *legacy for generations to come.* I truly believe that those three things have been the cornerstone of my personal and career success. Just like we do in a corporation, the same applies to us personally and professionally: Our brand tells people who we are, and everything we do and say should follow that branding.

Founder and CEO of Heartland Payment Systems, Inc. Robert Owen Carr's brand includes ingenuity and stick-to-itiveness. When I asked him to share what he'd learned from the crucibles in his life, he shared the following:

If you have a well-thought-out plan and you stick to it and keep modifying it as you learn new things, it can be incredibly powerfully successful. That's the Heartland story. I started out with a model that made sense to me and kept running into one detour or roadblock or another, like anyone else. As you figure out how to get around those roadblocks, you're figuring out how to solve the problems that everybody else tries to solve, yet few are successful at doing. You become an overnight success after forty-three years.

In the words of one of the world's leading inspirational leaders Les Brown, *"In order to be successful, you must be willing to do the things today others won´t do, in order to have the things tomorrow others won´t have."* Whatever your brand, have the courage to protect it, nurture it, and follow it through, even when it would be easier to follow the crowd. As Zions Bancorporation CEO Harris Simmons shared, *"Don't be fickle and subject to the winds of what's convenient. Rather, be willing to speak the truth even when it's inconvenient."* Success rarely comes from settling for the ordinary—it comes when you risk the extraordinary.

#3 Find Your Own Voice

In a culture that shouts at us through social media, twenty-four hour news stations, and various entertainment outlets, it is vital to know your own voice. Each person on this planet is unique and has a depth of distinctive experience, life lessons, and talents to offer. I love what Vice Admiral Raquel C. Bono of the US Navy had to say when I asked her what advice she had for up-and-coming leaders:

You need to become a student of yourself and hone a sense of self-awareness. You need to understand who you are, both in your emotional and intellectual make-up. Every interaction will test you, and your buttons will be pushed. Taking the time to understand whom you are is a worthy investment. When I embraced my own voice, I was able to relate more fully with people and be more effective in influencing them.

Dr. Andrew Benton shared the story of how he came to become president of Pepperdine University. His mentor and the former president David Davenport expressed concern that he would not enjoy the job, especially the pomp and circumstance of being a figurehead. He knew Dr. Benton was all about substance. On his first day as president, he made it clear that he knew his own voice and would proceed in his new role accordingly:

On June 16, 2000, I called a staff meeting and I said, "Listen, here's the deal. I'm going to be president my way. Not like Batsell Baxter, not like Hugh Tiner, not like Norvel Young, not like Bill Banowsky, not like Howard White, not like David Davenport. I have to do it my own way or it's going to lack authenticity. People will see through me so quickly. So hang on, it's going to be me, and I have to have a lot of students in my life. I need contact with faculty and with students, and donors will of course be of interest to me. I will do more than my share when it comes to fundraising and friend-raising, but at the end of the day they're just people, and what this institution is really about is changing lives."

As you develop your leadership style and develop relationships with people in both your life and career, you will find your voice. It may be the calm, steady voice of reason or the passionate, rallying voice of changing the world. When you know and understand yourself better, you will be better equipped to relate with and positively influence others.

#4 Seek Out Champions

Mentors will help you along the way as you grow in your leadership journey; CHAMPIONS will put their reputation on the line for you.

When I was starting my career as Manager of the El Toro branch at Wells Fargo, I became the first female Rotarian officer in the local Rotary Club. There I found my first mentor. Tom Timmons, CEO of a small bank in Orange County, took the time to teach me how to think like a CEO. We met regularly throughout the years, and he even met with my staff as my role grew. Tom was the perfect mentor.

I have been fortunate to have many CHAMPIONS in my life. One of them was responsible for my first keynote speech in Beijing, China. Randy Hunt told the founder and CEO of the Maple Women's Society about my upcoming trip to China where I would be bringing 3,000 letters from kids around America for kids in Sichuan who had lost their parents in the earthquake that shook the country. I received an invitation to be the keynote speaker at their 20th year anniversary—little did I know that Hillary Clinton was the keynote speaker for their 19th year anniversary! Randy put his reputation on the line, and based on HIS brand, I became the keynote speaker and was able to add value and build trust clear across the world. Randy was the perfect champion.

Your champions will seek out opportunities for your career and will put their reputation on the line for you. They will honor your values and support you in making the right decisions. Take the time to seek out your champions.

#5 Inspire Other Leaders to Be the Best Versions of Themselves

As a values-based leader, one of your strongest motivations to lead will be empowering other up-and-coming leaders to be better, more courageous, more in tune with their driving purpose in life. I know that I have been on the receiving end of such inspiration, and it is a privilege to mentor and inspire others in the same way. I talked earlier in the book about a very tangible way that one of the executives I interviewed inspires his leaders toward greatness. Founder and CEO David Long of MyEmployees has made it his personal mission to grow his people, creating value and establishing true buy-in, with his book club program. Inspiring his people to be the best version of themselves is one of his primary goals as CEO. In his own book *Built to Lead*, David shares one of his favorite quotes by Zig Ziglar: "You can have everything in life that you want, if you help enough people get what they want." Inspiring others and reaching back to pull them up will not deplete you or demote you; on the contrary, inspiring others will both fulfill you and lift you up, helping you align with your own life purpose.

General Julie Bentz, PhD, has both led in military settings and worked under two presidential administrations; she understands more than most how important it is to inspire future leaders.

During our interview, she transitioned from speaking about high-level international strategic positioning to remembering her time as a missionary and explaining how that skill set factors into her current role.

> *I found myself caring for people. In the hierarchical environment of real life, one can very much be the servant of the ones they lead. I was responsible for their welfare, responsible for their feeling of usefulness, responsible for them finding their purpose. This was an exciting time, one that evoked out of my deepest core a feeling of, "I'm doing something that I was built to do."*

Today she has the immensely demanding responsibility of coordinating tactical strategies for troops facing dire threats abroad on a daily basis. Dr. Julie Bentz gets excited when she helps someone find their purpose and inspires them to, like her, find something they were "built to do." I am reminded of my dear friend and community leader CEO Matt Toledo of the LA Business Journal as he speaks of helping people figure out what they want to do in relation to knowing their goals:

> *I think it's tremendously motivating for people when you take an interest in them, help them figure out what they want, and you help them get it. It really boils down to a goals issue. When you know what you want in life, every minute of every day you're doing things that are engaged in getting that. If you don't know what you want, then you have to manage your time among things that are just not relevant. I did a Google search a couple of years back on the subject and there were around 3,000 books on the subject of time management and*

only a couple of hundred on goal setting. I thought to myself that lack of goal setting is the problem. If people knew what their goals were, there wouldn't be time management issues, but somehow we've gotten all jacked up on this culture of time management when we should really be educating people on the subject of what do they want in life.

Matt Toledo's mission is to inspire others, then helping them articulate and execute their goals. He knows from years of experience that when people know what they want, they are virtually unstoppable in achieving their goals. He was recently awarded the "Mentor of The Year" award from Pepperdine University for the difference he has made for many people in reaching their goals.

I could list story after story shared in my interviews because each and every one of the high-level leaders I spoke with valued their people enough to inspire them to be better. This one idea is embodied in every one of the leaders who are highlighted in this book. In my dissertation study, the subjects' motivation to lead was: creating value for others, impacting change, mentoring others, personal achievement, purpose in life, and taking care of others. The very purpose and resolve that gets them out of bed in the morning is centered not on themselves but on others. That should speak volumes to us as leaders.

Let's face it. Our lives are continuously evolving; and as such, so are we. As our situations change, our tools for handling life and leadership situations should also continue to evolve. In order for us to inspire others to be the best version of themselves, we must lead by example and do the same for ourselves; this is accomplished through our own growth and development as leaders.

#6 Leave a Legacy

I have spoken in this book at length about leaving a legacy. At first, my legacy was for my children like my mother and father left behind for my brothers and me when they passed away. But my life purpose has now grown to include leaving a legacy of values-based leaders in every continent in the world. I shared earlier in the book how I want to have a positive impact in the world by igniting a spark of values-based leadership in heads of state, CEOs and their spheres of influence, and students of leadership. Through hard work, passion and determination, my values proposition and influence have already begun to expand to every continent. I have traveled to Kenya with the Unstoppable Foundation, where I visited with students who are recipients of my scholarship fund, which I am funding with the proceeds of the sale of this book and my speaking engagements. I have also formed a partnership with Bob Carr and the Give Something Back Foundation to provide scholarships in North America. I spoke to Dr. Lopez who is interested in collaborating to provide scholarships for underserved students in Colombia, South America. And so, by aligning my purpose with my actions, doors continue to open. (Can you believe it? He found me on LinkedIn!!)

What about you … what is the legacy you want to leave?

Maybe you want to leave a legacy of courage, initiating change in places no one else will go. Perhaps you want to leave a legacy of integrity, daring to buck the status quo in favor of living an authentic life.

Dr. Andrew K. Benton, President of Pepperdine University is really engaging with his students and leading with heart. Compassionate by nature, Dr. Benton ("Andy" to his former students and AKB to current students) cares deeply for the university and the role it plays in the lives of its students.

> *I lead with heart and conviction. Heart is really important for me, so I'm willing to be more transparent, more available, more authentic. That is very fulfilling for me. Everything that I do, really, is about students. I think that's as it should be. I love faculty research, and I love faculty, but at the end of the day I believe in what George Pepperdine established; he believed in the impact that education could have on the hearts and minds of men and women. I often wonder if I am getting it right; am I keeping faith with what he had in mind? With all that in mind, it's heart, conviction, keeping faith and traction with the dream—I hope that will be my legacy.*

Leaving a legacy is about looking forward and adjusting your current actions in order to influence the future. Robert Louis Stevenson says, "Don't judge each day by the harvest you reap but by the seeds that you plant." Those seeds that you plant now—integrity, courage, growth, personal responsibility—will grow into the legacy that continues to flourish long after you are gone.

#7 Don't Ever, Ever Forget Where You Came From – Step into the Light

This is about humility. Sometimes I sit in board rooms filled with executives, some of whom have grown to believe the lie. By that I mean, they believe they are their title. I often tell my people how much I dislike titles; while they open doors outside the company (people will see you with open arms if your title is high enough), they build walls inside the company (people will tell you what you want to hear because you are the "big boss.").

Just as important as it is to look to the future, we must never forget where we started. I shared earlier in the book how I made my first values-based decision to come to America with my mother, leaving behind the comfort and financial security of my father's home in Colombia. I have never forgotten where I came from, and it has changed the way I operate. I *work harder.* I worked two jobs while putting myself through college as a single mother. I *study longer.* The longest was the last six months of my dissertation when my weekend writings began at 6:00 a.m. and ended around 11:00 p.m. Saturdays and Sundays, and my week days were full of writing before and after work from 3:30 a.m. to 7:00 a.m. and from 7:00 p.m. to midnight. It is always important to remember where you came from and allow your unique experience to influence you for the better.

Many of the study participants experienced challenging circumstances that led to difficult starts in life, but they chose to use those challenges as fuel to go further and do more. Earlier in the book, I shared how CEO Robert Bard of *Latina Style Magazine* rediscovered his heritage through a mentor relationship. Through his pursuit of success in business, he had forgotten where he came from. Fully embracing his roots brought him both unexpected fulfillment and the welcome byproduct of success.

Chairwoman of ProAmerica Bank Maria Salinas shared how she has a soft spot for young Latinas starting off in the business and financial industries. When she gets a request for her time or mentorship, she remembers how much she would have valued that kind of input and she always answers with an enthusiastic Yes! Never forgetting where you came from means that 1) you value the people who supported you in your journey, 2) you seek a posture of humility and compassion with others, and 3) you reach back and bring others with you.

Leading from a position of humility makes you stronger, not weaker. As you navigate your life and leadership journey, never forget where you came from.

#8 Trust Your Instincts

In his book *Leadership Beyond Reason*, best-selling author of *Boundaries* Dr. John Townsend introduces the idea that leaders make decisions based on both their internal and external worlds. "You, as a leader, are probably more trained, prepared, and experienced in the external world than you are in the internal one. Most likely, you are able to amass large amounts of valuable information from reports, research, journals, and interviews. And you need that information; it is critical to your success as a leader. At the same time, you also need access to data within you that is just as valuable and helpful to how you lead, come to conclusions, and make decisions."[35]

We have all experienced that pit-of-the-stomach feeling when confronted with a possible business venture, growth opportunity, mission objective, or any other endeavor that involves a component of risk. Founder and CEO of Heartland Payment Systems, Inc. Robert Owen Carr who successfully sold his company for $4.3 Billion, shared that he has made three big mistakes in his life, despite being very successful, and he should have trusted his instincts in each situation.

> *You don't have to play the cards you are dealt. What do I mean by that? Just because you've been put into a set of circumstances that are uncomfortable and are going to put unrealistic burdens on you, you don't have to accept that. In each situation, I wasn't willing to put everything at risk to confront the problem. The only reason I went through all the problems I did was because I was not strong enough to confront others about what my instincts told me we should do. I finally learned my lesson, but it was a very expensive, hard lesson. I spent about twenty-five years of my life digging out of these problems and made much less progress as a result.*

It has been my experience that my intuition is rarely misguided. According to Malcom Gladwell's research, it takes 10,000 hours to become an expert. This expertise is often called intuition. Trust your intuition and have the strength to follow it, even if it means confronting an uncomfortable situation.

Have you ever interviewed someone who looked absolutely too perfect for the job? Not long ago, I interviewed someone for a senior management position and, although this person seemed perfect, I felt reservations that made me question … is the person too perfect? As usual in my interview process, I asked members of my senior staff to conduct interviews and they seemed impressed. Even then my "intuition" told me that it wasn't a perfect match, and I should look deeper. After a more thorough investigation, I decided not to hire this person. When you lead with your gut instincts, coupled with all the rational data available, success is far more likely.

#9 Live a Life of Gratitude

Most days I wake up with a smile on my face and a word of thanks for the opportunity I have to make a difference. But I'm not alone. Values-centered leaders tend to do just this. But how do they do it?

In a *Forbes* article on the power of gratitude in leadership, author of *The Trust Edge* David Horsager calls gratitude "the most powerful forgotten weapon." He goes on to share the research by Bersin & Associates on employee recognition: companies that "excel at employee recognition" are twelve times more likely to enjoy strong business results. In addition, his own academic findings on trust have led him to the conclusion that not only does gratitude make a difference, but people don't require big gestures, just heartfelt ones. Simple but genuine thank-yous or small, handwritten notes of appreciation can mean the world to people.[36]

One day while visiting branches, I encountered a Financial Services Representative who brought a very large relationship to the bank. My first instinct was to take her by the hand and walk with her to the local California Pizza Kitchen restaurant across the street and break bread with her in gratitude for a job well done. We talked about her children, one of whom was about to enter the university for the first time, and we compared notes with my own daughters who were attending Pepperdine and UCCS. She was overjoyed with the gesture, and her manager told me two days later what an impact that simple lunch had on her, saying it is rare to see an Executive Vice President getting to know people "at that level." The next time I saw her, she mentioned the impact our personal talk had in her daughter's life. I made a difference!

How many times have a few simple words or a gesture of appreciation from a friend or colleague bolstered you through a difficult challenge or encouraged you to reach higher and be more than you thought possible? When people feel that they are seen and understood, they become more engaged, and trust is simply a natural byproduct. Gratitude leads to trust, and trust leads to success. It is a choice, and you make it every day when you decide how you will think. As Greg Jacobson says, We can move ourselves from fear to awareness, anger to focus, disappointment to reflection, and satisfaction to active happiness and joy—simply by changing our thoughts, or choosing what to think in any situation." There is nothing you cannot accomplish when your people trust you, and you trust your people. When you combine that with living in gratitude, you become unstoppable.

CEO David Long's has built a thriving company, MyEmployees, on the idea of gratitude and recognition. The company's white paper on frontline employee engagement states, "The bottom-line success of your company may well depend on how engaged your frontline employees are with your company, their boss, and their work, because their level of engagement predicts how well they engage your customers."[37] This idea is not limited to the business world, however. Recognition is a concept that flourishes in every industry, every organization, every community and every family. Think of the scouts with their badges and the military with their medals. Recognition says, "I see you, and what you are doing matters to me."

Raul Salinas, Chairwoman Maria Salinas' husband shared that Maria is highly community minded, just as he is, and that she is fundamentally driven to make the world a better place. *"Maria's education was forged through a Jesuit philosophy. She went to Loyola Marymount University, where they have a sense of academic excellence as well as a deep-seated community involvement that is rooted in you by the time you leave the university. We're not overly religious, it's just in the sense of feeling that we're blessed. Gratitude. That's what motivates her."* Through their community involvement, they have created organizations that reach the Latino community, lifting up leaders and giving the marginalized a voice. Gratitude is indeed a powerful tool.

#10 Lead with a Higher Purpose

I end with the idea of leading with a higher purpose in my top ten guiding principles. What is a higher purpose? In my study I saw this as something bigger than you; an overarching purpose under which you align all of your actions, vision and purpose. Some of you reading this book will connect with your "why." Why did you choose to go in your particular field?

Vice Admiral Raquel Bono chose to operate on the soldier in the midst of bullets flying all around her; in the midst of battle and fear, she centered herself with her original reason to join the Navy: to make an impact on people and to save lives. That was her "higher purpose" which allowed her to save that soldier's life while missiles were flying all around her. She was clear on why she was there at that very moment.

As I learned through my research and you have learned throughout this book, those who lead with a higher purpose are able to inspire others to follow; this is because they are up to something bigger than themselves; bigger than just increasing profits in their company. While this is a very important part of a leader's job, aligning their people's jobs to a higher purpose is certainly what creates the "magic" in the job.

I remember my mother coming home one day and telling me about her purpose in her job. At the time, she worked in an assembly line, making "fasteners" (fancy name for screws). Prior to this day, if someone asked her what she did for a living, she said, "I make fasteners." Once the president of the company presented his vision to his employees, he told the assembly workers that the fasteners they made went on the space shuttle, and explained how important it was that all the fasteners were manufactured correctly. After that, my mother went around saying: "I work for the Space Shuttle!" She and her co-workers were very careful to make sure every part they made was completed in excellence—they had a higher purpose. As leaders, it is our responsibility to ensure everyone on our team knows the purpose of our organization, and it is clear and aligned with the values that govern our world. But this does not only apply to our professional life; it expands to our personal life as well. My mother used to say, "Dime conquien andas y te dire quien eres," or, "Tell me who you're with and I'll tell you who you are." In life, it is important to surround ourselves with professionals and individuals who are aligned with our purpose and values; whether we are hiring or appointing someone, alignment is key.

When we are clear about what we value most and align our actions with our values, the right situation comes around, the right team, the right people, and even the right partner.

The more we live and lead with purpose, the happier and more fulfilled we will be. Major General Angie Salinas feels that kind of purpose and passion for what she does and she happily shared the adage, "If you have a passion for what you do, you will never work a day in your life." Lt. General Mick Kicklighter fulfills his purpose in being a servant leader. CEO David Long fulfills his purpose in creating value for his people through book clubs. Raul and Maria Salinas fulfill their higher purpose in serving their community. Dr. Andrew Benton fulfills his purpose in connecting with and genuinely engaging with students at Pepperdine University. Matt Toledo fulfills his purpose in helping others fulfill their purpose.

You only live this life once, and my hope is to live it well. I love the advice CEO Matt Toledo had for up-and-coming leaders, fellow CEOs, and heads of state:

> *Here's my view. Be engaged. It's one time in this world and so while I'm here on this planet, while I'm here at this company, while I'm here as a daddy, as a family, I want to experience, achieve, taste, touch, and smell as much as I possibly can and that requires engagement. That's me in a nutshell.*

Julie Bentz, Ph.D. says it this way:

> *I have an eternal soul, and I'm here on this earth for a teeny piece of that. So my attitude is this—I'm going to live it to the hilt. Go for broke, man! We've got an average of seventy years, and I've only got twenty more*

years left. Go for broke. All the great saints throughout generations just did what the Lord told them to do, They just went for it. You can't tell me they didn't live the abundant life. And they all died early. Hot dog! Not a bad deal. Go for broke.

I absolutely love that. Go for broke. Give your all. Be engaged. Identify your own top ten and don't waver from them. As you begin to discover and live out your values, incorporating these principles along the way, you will better navigate your life and leadership journey wherever it takes you.

QUESTIONS TO KEEP YOU THINKING

1. What are your own "Top Ten?"

2. What is one way that you can begin leaving a legacy today?

3. What does living and leading with a higher purpose mean to you?

CHAPTER SUMMARY – Key Takeaways

* The first step to becoming a values-based leader is *knowing* your values, and the second is *following* them without exception.

* Dr. Betty's Top Ten:

    1. Lead With Values

    2. Protect Your Brand

    3. Find Your Own Voice

4. Seek Out Champions

5. Inspire Others to Be the Best Version of Themselves

6. Leave a Legacy

7. Don't Ever, Ever Forget Where You Came From

8. Trust Your Instincts

9. Be in Gratitude

10. Lead With a Higher Purpose

CHAPTER ELEVEN

We Don't Do This Alone

If I can see further,
it's because I'm standing on the shoulders of giants.
—Isaac Newton

When you read a book, you learn about the protagonist as you follow their hero's journey through the pages of the book. You may get glimpses into the thoughts and motivations of the supporting characters along the way, but they are not as highlighted or mentioned as those of the main character. They simply serve their purpose in the background, far from the glow of the limelight. However, the actions and motivations of the supporting characters are still vitally important to the success of the protagonist. Without them, the hero would never complete his journey, the heroine would never succeed in her quest.

I've always felt that it is important to go back and acknowledge the people who support us. *Behind every great leader is a great support team.* Like the hero or heroine in a story, great leaders would not be where they are today without the consistent encouragement of their loved ones, friends, mentors, and colleagues who support them throughout their journey.

With all of my heart I value those people who have supported me along the way, so much so that I end every meeting with the words: "We don't do this alone. Go and thank the people who support you in doing this work every day—your spouse, children, mentor, assistant, partner, support team, etc. This can be accomplished by writing a simple note, purchasing a single flower or some other token of your appreciation. Make sure they know that you value them."

As I began compiling the resources for this book and talking to people about their career journeys, it dawned on me that we rarely hear about the spouse and support systems of these great leaders. I felt that there was something to investigate in that respect, so I began to ask those I interviewed if I could speak with their spouses and support staff. Many were surprised, but they agreed to allow me to speak with their significant others, perhaps with a humble recognition of the part they truly played in their overall success. I knew that I was on the right track when Debby Benton, wife of Dr. Andrew Benton of Pepperdine University, echoed my thoughts:

> *It is so important to remember those who helped you along the way. She shared that Dr. Benton had done this just recently by writing ten or so letters to people who had influenced him in some way throughout his life. He wanted to thank them for helping him because he knew beyond a shadow of a doubt that he wouldn't be where he is today without their influence. He wanted to acknowledge in a tangible way that he remembered he didn't get there alone.*

How powerful is that?

When you stop to thank and acknowledge the people who have supported, encouraged, and mentored you, it has an amazing ripple effect. By reaching back with recognition and gratitude, you pull them up with you.

Whether you are a high-level executive leading a multi-billion dollar organization, a government leader in charge of a country or a state, an emerging leader, or student of leadership, your success did not come without the support of those around you, propping you up as you chased your dreams. They are our support system, re-centering us on what matters, serving as our anchor when the inevitable storms of life batter us, and being there for us as our private confidantes when we simply need someone to listen. Whatever role the supporting cast in your life play, it is so very important to lift up and acknowledge them—and do it often.

Vice Admiral Raquel Bono and her husband Art Dwight are shining examples of a successful narrative, where both characters play a supporting role in each other's stories. Their strong commitment, both to each other and to their respective career roles, is worthy of admiration. I have seen the great respect Art has for Raquel, who has been given the fitting nickname of "Rocky" Bono for her fierce determination and work ethic. You can hear his admiration as he describes Raquel in the chapters of his book, *Look at This*. He shares that her high standards for excellence originated with her parents, who taught her personal sacrifice, service to others, and most importantly hard work. In his words,

Rocky's family tradition of military and medical service instilled in her the importance of excellence at a young age. In both professions there is little margin for error—mistakes can cost lives. He goes on to say: "Excellence matters in everything whether it's performing surgery, cleaning bathrooms, or how people treat each other."

Raquel Bono had to work harder, longer, and outperform her peers just to be considered equal. Art calls her a hundred-pound dynamo who not only defies stereotype but obliterates it, with the paradoxical combination of a combat officer with a heart of gold. She sees the standard as a minimum level of performance; the true standard for her was to bring out the very best of everyone in her command. *"When she backed up her words with action, without regard to personal consequences,"* Art says, *"they knew that they finally had a leader they could trust and believe in. Their faith in the Navy, and everything it represents was restored."* His support for her is palpable when he says of his amazing wife, *"Rocky taught me that uncompromising dedication to standards is not only possible but essential to elevate our life and the lives of others."* Raquel Bono and Art Dwight support each other, reaching back with recognition and gratitude, and pulling each other higher than they could go on their own.

This kind of support was evident across the board with study participants. I wish I could have spoken with each and every spouse and support team, because I know their stories would echo the same level of encouragement that I witnessed with Raquel Bono and her husband Art.

I was able to ask a few spouses and support teams of my interview subjects about their leader's motivation to lead, defining career moments, special rituals they created to stay close as a couple or team, and five pieces of advice that they would offer to those coming up in leadership and the ones who support them. It was clear that both the leaders and their support team had a high level of respect for each other, and the depth of support went both ways.

Our Supporters Know What Makes Us Tick

Chairwoman Maria Salinas spoke of her husband Raul Salinas as the one person who pushed her to believe in herself and aim higher. When she had the opportunity to do something that seemed out of reach, he gave her the courage to pursue it. Sometimes our supporters know us better than we know ourselves. They champion us and see all of the outstanding qualities that we may not be able to perceive clearly in ourselves. Raul Salinas, himself a successful attorney, partners with Maria and supports her in every endeavor. He glowed with pride when he spoke of his wife's leadership capability:

> *When it comes to her leadership role, she's prepared and not guided by personality, which is important. Her decision-making is analytical and in the best interest of the institution, even if it comes at the expense of relationships. I think that's a very hard, but very valuable characteristic to acquire, the ability to say hard truths and to make decisions based on hard truths. It's a very valuable skill that she possesses. She also has impeccable integrity, and she is the last one to want to draw attention to herself. She is not motivated*

by ego, and I think people see that in her. It's easy to rally around her, as it is easy to rally around any leader when people feel that they are in it for everyone and not just for their own personal gain.

They share a love of serving the community and have made an enormous impact on the local community as a result by creating and serving non-profit organizations that serve Latino professionals. They have made it a habit to live out the idea of *mi casa es su casa*, regularly inviting others into their home to break bread, connect, and genuinely engage with people. Despite their busy schedules, relationships are a priority, and they invest in that value. Raul and Maria both live by the philosophy that you can do well in life by doing good. Raul shared, *"The good we've done in the community has led to our personal satisfaction, a beautiful marriage, and it has also led to development with professional relationships that have helped us with our careers."* There is a beautiful balance to their personal and professional lives that works for them. When you find a similar balance with your closest family and most valued advisors, you are able to be the best version of yourself as a leader.

As high-level leaders, we can often become workaholics, taking our careers with us into every space of life. Our loved ones and supporters intuitively know when we need to distance ourselves from our work—when it becomes all-encompassing and detracts from our effectiveness as leaders.

Wife of CEO David Long, Janet Long, shared that she grounds her husband emotionally, always stands by his side during tough times, and strives to create balance for him. When they first started the business, she would go into the company and run the office. It wasn't easy to do while taking care of little children, whom she chose to take to the office daily as the work had to be done. She has been David's biggest fan, through thick and through thin. She even moved into her mother-in-law's home when they were close to being completely broke. Today, the employees of their company have the utmost care and respect for her.

In my own life, I have had many supporters joining me and supporting me all the way to the finish line. When I was completing my doctorate, Juan Carlos often joined me for a weekend away from the distractions of everyday life so that I could finish my dissertation; he supported me emotionally when there was little left of me to give. My friend Clemencia and her husband brought me a pot of homemade chili and reminded me that they were praying for me. They also celebrated with me when I completed my doctoral work with a "Welcome Back, Betty" party! You need these type of people in your life for balance and a truly fulfilling life. Value them for the treasures they are to you.

President of Pepperdine University Dr. Andrew Benton's wife Debby shared that sometimes her supportive role has been subtle, serving as a welcome distraction from the rigors and stress of leading a prestigious university.

> *Sometimes he gets very "one-track-minded." He decides he's going to do something, and that's all he thinks about. We all understand that need for balance in life, to have other things going on besides work and career. I decided that as his wife I needed to be his biggest distraction. He cares so deeply about the university, he's a bit of a workaholic. I'm constantly finding things to do, get away for a weekend, even just talk about ordinary non-work things, and that helps*

him. Sometimes you need to get away from whatever you're dealing with in order to see more clearly. Debby Benton's Leadership Advice: Perspective is everything. When you take a step back from a problem or issue and disengage for a while, that is sometimes when the answers and deeper clarity come.

Debby shared one ritual that creates balance and a sense of intimacy in everyday life—eating at least one meal together every day. Though she admits that it is not always possible to eat together because of both of their responsibilities to the university, they talk at least once a day. *"We stay open and communicate constantly about everything. We talk often and try our best to be there for each other. Absence doesn't always make the heart grow fonder—sometimes it just makes you more independent, which can be a good and bad thing. We try to do things together rather than apart as much as possible."*

When I asked her to describe her husband, this is what she said: *"He is shy, was always a leader from the time he was a student; he has a quiet way about him, very wise. He has always had a level of maturity; he wasn't silly like some of the other boys, which is what initially attracted me to him. He is considerate, kind, substantive, involved in important things and full of kindness."* These are the words of a woman who admires her man.

She knows her husband and best friend better than anyone else, and she supports him unconditionally. She shared, *"Men and women who are leaders need to be independent, but they need to know that there's someone that always supports them, even if they don't always agree with them. In any marriage, two people are not going to agree on everything. You must always respect each other's thoughts and beliefs."* Your supporters may not agree with everything you do or say, but they will be aligned with your core values and support you in the execution of those values.

I will never forget the day I met Lt. General Mick Kicklighter, "The General," as his friends from the White House and the Pentagon fondly call him. We met at his favorite diner across the river from D.C., and his wife Betty joined us shortly thereafter. His office was in the Pentagon at that time. Anyone who knows Betty can see that she is beautiful, inside and out, and exudes confidence and ladylike eloquence. As she sat down next to him, she said, *"I just had to come over and see who you are, that my husband—who has never before granted an interview—decided to talk with you."* I couldn't help but wonder the same thing, but I was appreciative of the opportunity to get a rare glimpse into this couple's unique relationship.

When you see Mick and Betty Kicklighter together, you can't help but fall in love with both of them. I have had the pleasure of breaking bread with them together... and individually. When they are together, he takes such good care of her, and she *allows* him to care for her. When they are away from each other, they are whole. She is self-sufficient, articulate, lovely, and a foundation upon which they have built a home for their family and each other. He has "bearing," a term coined by the military, which includes professional appearance, confidence, courteous, and having a positive outlook. Based on my experience of him, I would add to this list: chivalry, selflessness, intellectual honesty, loyalty, and genuine care.

Among his pictures with presidents and heads of state hang pictures of the two of them together at different times in his career. Their relationship is solid, authentic, and built upon years of shared experience, shared values, and shared lives. She has been the pillar of the household. He had to travel a lot, as he was a general in the army over the Western United States to Eastern China; she held down the fort. While he traveled, she found comfort with other military wives as the military always provides a support system for families; she was never alone when he was away being the warrior fighting for freedom, and she was the safe place to come home to.

Their care for each other was palpable as he shared his stories and she interjected with "No, Mick, that's not quite how that happened. You're being too modest. This is what really happened..." I learned during that interview, and in the many subsequent meetings with these two gems, that these leaders are so humble. They don't see themselves as role models or heroes. They are just doing their jobs, yet their spouses know the truth of the sacrifices they make, the burdens they bear, and the battles they fight.

Your supporters know the same of you, and that is worthy of gratitude.

Your Supporters Share Wisdom for the Journey

In your direct sphere of influence, there is an abundance of wisdom hidden in the people around you. Many of the leaders I spoke with shared that they valued the perspectives and opinions of those on their boards, committees, and teams. I have discovered time and again in my life that every person has something unique to bring to the table. When I asked the spouses and supporters I interviewed for pieces of advice they would give to up-and-coming leaders, high-level CEOs, and heads of state, they shared some valuable pearls of wisdom.

Pearls of wisdom from Raul Salinas:

1. **Character is how you act when no one is looking.**

   A true leader will respond to a situation without regard to personal acclaim or seeking attribute but because it's the right thing to do. We all have weaknesses in our persona, everybody does. The value of a leader is to recognize those weaknesses, address them, and not fall prey to them. If you have seen leaders as you've studied them, they thought no one would see how they act.

2. **The tools belong to the man that uses them.**

   A corollary to that is that they have to be used correctly. You need to use the tools and gifts provided to you.

3. **To be effective as a leader, you have to learn to process.**

   So much of what we do in life is done on misinformation or miscalculation. Understand the process of whatever you want done—getting into college, doing community service, building a company from the ground up.

4. **To be an effective policy maker and leader, you have to empathize with the other side.**

   You need to understand them. What is so polemic in Washington right now is that no one is willing to understand the other side.

5. **You can do well in life by doing good.**

   I built my client base by doing community service and building genuine relationships. It has never been my intent to pursue law to make a lot of money. Money has come, but it was never the main motivation. It was to help the community from which I came. That's my defining legacy. When I talk to young attorneys about that, I stress that what matters is how successful you are from doing good.

Each of these pieces of advice could be expanded into one entire chapter in this book. No wonder Maria Salinas has been so successful, with a husband who shares her values and purpose, filled with depth and character, who wouldn't be inspired to reach the very top!

Pearls of wisdom from Debby Benton:

1. **Humility is huge**. No one likes to see someone's ego front and center.

2. **Remember those who helped you along the way**.

    A few years ago Andy did this (and I decided to do this as well). He wrote about ten people to thank them for helping him because he wouldn't be where he is today without their influence. One of them was an English teacher. It's about remembering that you didn't get there alone.

3. **Don't exclusively surround yourself only with people in power**. You need a diverse section of friends to keep you grounded.

4. **If you are married, make time for each other, doing simple little things**.

    The best memory I have of Andy was when he drove out to a hotel where I was making a speech simply to take the time to give me a hug and a kiss. My first thought was "Oh no—I don't want him to be in the audience." When he told me he had come just to wish me luck and let me know he believed in me, that was a memorable moment. When it comes to family, it's not always the big gestures. Sometimes it's the small ones.

5. **Enjoy every moment**. Sometimes you'll be looking forward to this or that, but it's the journey.

> You're out in these leadership roles. There are a lot of things that you don't expect. We've gotten to meet Margaret Thatcher, the Reagans, the Bushes. Enjoy the surprises along the way. The little things are BIG. As leaders, we need to take time to enjoy them instead of looking to the next big thing.

I especially like that last piece of advice. My mother used to say, "Look at the little things; that's where the treasures are, in the little things." Life is about moments. When we take the time to really take in those moments and be grateful *at the moment,* we are present in that moment and take it in. That's what life truly is about.

Pearls of wisdom from Lupita Colmenero:

Here's a look behind the curtain on Robert Bard and his wife Lupita. They work together, live together, and maintain a sacred space for their relationship as a couple and with their children.

Lupita Colmenero is the wife of Robert Bard, CEO of *LATINA Style* magazine, the largest magazine of its kind across the nation. She is an accomplished leader in her own right, as she owns *El*

Hispano newspaper in Dallas, and is the president, CEO, and founder of a non-profit in Dallas, *Parents Step Ahead,* which Robert vice-chairs. As you can imagine, they are both very busy. Robert is on the board of the US Navy and travels across the country for the magazine, doing forums for business women and educating them about how to grow their businesses. Lupita also pours her heart and time into her community through Parents Step Ahead, the organization she founded to remedy the growing lack of awareness plaguing parents, especially underserved parents, which has put their children at a significant disadvantage in school and in life.

When I had the opportunity to speak with her, she had so much wisdom to offer leaders regarding health, balance, and vitality, and I wanted to share a few here in these pages.

1. **Equip yourself for every occasion**. When asked how she and her husband manage to do it all, Lupita responded that it is just like choosing the right outfit for an occasion. You wear it until the event is finished, and then you prepare yourself properly for the next one. In other words, you "put on" the energy you need and just get it done!

2. **Keep your home sacred**. Robert and Lupita do something that is almost unheard of in this frenzied, technology-driven world. When they walk through the doors of their home, business shuts down. There is no working, although there is a computer for emergencies. Instead of staying tied to their respective careers in the evenings, they truly unplug in order to savor the time together cooking and spending time with the children. *They guard their sanctuary.*

3. **Take care of yourself**. Something she reminded me of when we spoke is that airlines caution you to put on your

oxygen mask first, then to help others around you. If you don't take care of yourself, you will have nothing left to give others. Lupita makes it a point to get at least seven hours of sleep per night, sometimes ten on the weekends, and this practice leads to a better mood, brighter spirits, greater energy, and even younger skin! This is her secret for staying young and beautiful, even with the tremendous demands on her time.

Every leader can benefit from incorporating more wisdom into their lives, and I truly hope that the words of these phenomenal leaders have inspired you to reach higher, be more thoughtful in your daily routine, and love more deeply.

Your Supporters Help You Build Your Legacy

Whether family, friends, or colleagues, those who support you in your life and leadership roles are the very first emissaries of your legacy. As you find your purpose and step into the light, they come alongside you and help spread your legacy to the world.

As I mentioned in chapter one of this book, I experienced a piece of my legacy demonstrated just recently when my daughter sent me a letter she had written for a university class. In it, she thanked me for all of the sacrifices I had made as a mother when she was young in order to achieve my dreams and provide a better life for my children. There is no greater gift as a parent than knowing you have made a difference in your child's life. I would like to share some of that letter with you now:

Dear Mom,

I remember the first time you told me the story. It was getting close to my twelfth birthday and you wanted to share with me why that age was so significant to you. You told me that it was at that same age that you came to America from Colombia. I could tell that it was something that was extremely important to you, but at that time I didn't realize how significant it truly was. Recently you sent me the story from your point of view. I don't think I could really fully understand the significance of what you did for me until much later. It is for this reason that I wanted to take the time to officially thank you for what you have done for me. Words cannot describe how much you mean to me and how thankful I am for your sacrifice but with this letter, I will try.

Growing up, you worked a lot and I resented that. I would cry when you left for your business trips and would continue to be sad until you returned. I realize now that you didn't have a choice. You were just doing your job and providing for our broken family just as you have done for your whole life. I was ungrateful and I apologize for that. You came to this country with practically nothing but the clothes on your back and made a name for yourself. You later married my dad and had my sister and me. Then, when tragedy struck, you were forced to up and leave once again. It is these difficult decisions that made me realize how strong you are and I thank you for that.

I want to thank you for raising my sister and me the way you did and for always trying to be there for us. You are my role model and I am so thankful for all of the sacrifices you have made for us. I look at the family we have in Colombia and how the women there are treated so poorly and I think, "That could've been me had it not been for your strength and sacrifice." You could have easily decided to stay with your dad whom you loved so dearly but instead you chose to come to America. Ever since then you have fought to make a name for yourself and to make a difference for those around you and I admire you so much for that.

As I am in college now and starting a new chapter in my life, I realize how different my life could have been. Without you, every aspect of my life would be so different. I would most likely not be getting a college education right now. I want to thank you for not only providing me with the opportunity to go to college, but also for instilling in me the importance of getting an education and the drive to be better.

You are my role model and I want to thank you from the bottom of my heart for the sacrifices you made to come to this country. You are the strongest person I know and you have this determination within you to make a difference for those around you that is inspiring. Your love of life and appreciation for everything that you have is contagious and I love that about you. You have been through so much in your life, yet you continue striving to be a better person each and every day. You have taught me what it is to forgive through your actions and not just your words. I will always remember something you used to say when I was younger. "La vida es linda sabiendola vivir." Life is beautiful knowing how to live it. Because of you, I can see the beauty in life. I love you so much and I hope that you know just how thankful I am for everything you have done for me.

Words cannot describe the feeling I had that night while reading her email. I cried tears of joy and thanked God for giving me the wisdom to be the head of my household while I was raising them. I was overwhelmed with gratitude seeing my own daughter practice a principle of gratitude that is so near and dear to my heart. Being the recipient of such gratitude is so very humbling and empowering.

You have not gotten to where you are on your own. Take the time to identify the people in your life and leadership journey who have supported and lifted you up. Thank them for what they have done. As you identify the supporting characters in the pages of your life's journey and elevate them with gratitude, you yourself will be elevated. As you sow gratitude and love in the people around you, the resulting harvest is true prosperity—the kind that is not measured in dollars and cents.

Every one of the people highlighted in this chapter supported their protagonists, and without them, the journey would not have been the same. It is important to recognize that trusting others to support us is a sign of strength and wisdom. So many times we fail to reach out as leaders, yet it is in the company of greatness that greatness occurs. Every global role model has had their supporters;

Jesus had his twelve disciples; Mother Theresa had her followers; Gandhi had his supporters. The way for us to duplicate ourselves is by opening up to the possibility that *we don't do this alone*. It takes a village, and that village is right in our backyard.

CONCLUSION

If you've made it this far in the book, I want to say *thank you*. I wish that I could take you by the hand, lead you to a local restaurant, and break bread with you, as I have done with so many others who have been a part of my journey. I want you to know that your values matter. Your decisions matter.

YOU matter.

Remember the story of Craig Kielburger, co-founder of "Free the Children"? His story shows what is truly possible when leaders completely align their values with their actions. This man is not even forty years old, yet he is making a difference in literally hundreds of people's lives around the world. Over twenty years ago, he and his brother set out on a bold mission to work with developing communities to free children and their families from poverty and exploitation. Through their work, they have developed a sustainable strategy to do just that, revolving around education. Today the parents are seeing the benefit of an education and are very emphatic about their kids going to school. When asked what is more important, clean water or education, the parents said education is more important. Amazing! Of the brothers' work, Sir Richard Branson says, "What they've accomplished is truly remarkable. They've inspired a generation of young people to care and set an example for all of us."[38]

And it all started with putting action to their #Values.

There is a reason that you opened this book, and my hope is that you will take what you have learned in these pages about values and duplicate it in every situation, every boardroom, every committee—every single interaction in your life and career.

I encourage you to think, talk about, and share your values with everyone you know. Live your life authentically, with your values center-stage every day, through every challenge, and with every decision. Be someone who lives and works within a values-driven paradigm, choosing to have alignment and balance in your life. As Stephen Covey says, "Personal leadership is the process of keeping your vision and values before you and aligning your life to be congruent with them." This is your life's work now, consistently aligning your life to be congruent with your values.

You have heard some of my story and the success stories of many others who have led with values in good times and bad with integrity, compassion, a hunger for learning and growing, and a passion to ignite change.

Now it's your turn.

I challenge you to strive to create value for others. Take the time to invest in them, help them discover their wants, and ignite that passion and excitement that makes them *want* to do well and work harder for you as their leader. Start building trust with your colleagues, both above and below your position. Mentor someone, and ask someone to mentor you. Never stop learning and growing.

You are equipped with the strategies to make a difference in your sphere of the world—whether as a head of state, C-level executive, military leader, or community leader—and I encourage you to see yourself as the protagonist of your own story.

YOU can be a leader whose actions are congruent with your espoused values.

YOU can lead with integrity and intellectual honesty.

YOU can focus on the good of the whole.

YOU can make a positive impact in others.

Now that you know about values-centered leadership, I pass the torch to you. I challenge you to go out into your world, in your area of influence, and share your unique strengths and talents, always putting your values first. The journey is never easy, but it is what shapes you and refines you into who you are meant to be in this life. Don't settle for the easy way. Strive for the best way.

Together, we can change the world with #Values—One person at a time.

ABOUT THE AUTHOR

Dr. Betty Uribe
and
#Values: The Secret to Top Level Performance in
Business and Life
by Pablo Schneider and Kristin Schneider

Arriving in the United States from Colombia at the age of twelve and not speaking any English, Betty Uribe's first job was cleaning houses to help support her family. Fast forward to today, and Dr. Betty Uribe is a nationally and internationally renowned senior banking executive, entrepreneur, speaker and author. The secret to her success? Values-based leadership.

In her remarkable life journey, "Dr. Betty" has touched the lives of thousands upon thousands of people around the world. From humble beginnings, her journey has included our God, family, and friends at the center of her life; impacting companies and communities throughout her twenty-eight-year banking career; earning four college degrees; owning five small businesses; and serving on the boards of several private, educational, and non-profit organizations.

Early on, Dr. Betty recognized that the world was crying out for better leadership. She had achieved significant success but at the same time realized that across societies, trust levels in leaders were dropping as more and more people became disillusioned and lost confidence in everyone from high-profile public figures, to CEOs, to political leaders. This realization, combined with having a heart for helping others succeed and for making the world a better place, sparked her pursuit of the secret to top-level performance in business and life—values-based leadership.

From diverse communities in North America, South America, and Asia, to African Massai Mara villages, to the Presidential Palace of Colombia, the White House, and the Vatican, Betty has engaged in values-based leadership with everyone from student leaders to world leaders. It became readily apparent there was a strong thread across diverse industries and walks of life. The most successful and trusted leaders all embodied strong, personal, higher values; they made decisions based on these values, and made a difference for others while living with a higher purpose. This translated into powerful, values-based leadership that propelled these leaders to succeed at the highest levels of society, and, equally as important, to succeed in their personal lives.

Dr. Betty began gathering the lessons she learned in her life, career, educational pursuits, and leadership activities, with the goal of helping others succeed in both their professional and personal lives. Thus was born the book, *#Values: The Secret to Top Level Performance in Business and Life.* In her book, Dr. Betty highlights the values and leadership strengths of some of the top culture-drivers in North America. #Values challenges the reader to ask themselves, *Can I be a better leader?* then provides the tools, advice, and encouragement needed to help people do just that. One leader at a time, Dr. Betty and *#Values* are effecting the transformation in America's and the world's culture, business environment, and human capital.

FIELD GUIDE: MORE ON #VALUES ·

In this book I highlighted leaders who lead with a higher set of values and who have achieved unprecedented results through the creation of a values-based culture in their organizations. My next book will provide a field guide that will show the reader "how" to create a values-based culture, utilizing proven models and templates that have been successfully utilized for culture creation. Stay tuned...

If you are moved to action and really want to help me make a positive in the world, here is how you can begin to PAY IT FORWARD. If you would like to make a difference for kids around the world, please go to www.drbettyuribe.com.

ENDNOTES

1 NOTES
http://pqdtopen.proquest.com/pubnum/3524029.
html?FMT=AI

2 http://www.bbc.com/news/world-us-canada-17747793

3 Rokeach, M. (1973). *The nature of human values.* New York, NY: The Free Press.

4 Charan, R. (2009). *Leadership in the era of economic uncertainty: The new rules for getting the right things done in difficult times.* New York, NY: McGraw Hill.

5 Schwartz, S. H., & Bilsky, W. (1987). Toward a universal psychological structure of human values. *Journal of Personality and Social Psychology, 53,* 550-562. Retrieved from http://psycnet.apa.org/index.cfin?fa=buy.optionToBuy&id=1988-01444-001

6 Schwartz, S. H. (1992). Universals in the content and structure of values: Theoretical advances and empirical tests in 20 countries. *Advances in Experimental Social Psychology, 25,* 1-65. doi:l0.1016/S0065-2601(08)60281-6

7 Covey, S. M. R. (2006, p. 11). *The speed of trust.* New York, NY: Free Press.

8 http://www.operationhope.org/hopeboardmember/sgc/10/c/71

9 Dyer, Dr. Wayne. *The Power of Intention.* Hay House Books, 2004.

10 Schein, Edgar H. Organizational Culture and Leadership. San Francisco, CA: Jossey-Bass, 2010.

11 Deal, Terrance E. & Kennedy, Allan A. The New Corporate Cultures: Revitalizing the Workplace after Downsizing, Mergers, and Reengineering. New York, NY: Basic Books, 1999.

12 Stogdill, R. M. (1974). *Handbook of leadership.* New York, NY: Free Press.

13 Stogdill, R. M. (1948). Personal factors associated with leadership: A survey of the literature. *Journal of Psychology, 25,* 35-71. Retrieved from http://www.mendeley.com/research/personal-factors-associated-with-leadership a-survey-of-the-literature/

14 Fiedler, F. E. (1967). *A theory of leadership effectiveness.* New York, NY: McGraw-Hill.

15 House, R. J. (1971). A path-goal theory of leader effectiveness. *Administrative Science Quarterly, 16,* 321-38.

16 Borgotta, E. G., Rouch, A. S., & Bales, R. F. (1954). Some findings relevant to the great man theory of leadership. *American Sociological Review, 19,* 755-759.

17 Pfeffer, J. (1981). *Power in Organizations.* Marshfield, MA: Pitman.

18 Mumford, M. D., Zaccaro, S. J., Harding, F. D., Jacobs, T. 0., & Fleishman, E. A. (2000). Leadership skills for a changing

world: Solving complex social problems. *Leadership Quarterly, 11(1)*, 11-35.

19 McGregor, D. (1966). *Leadership and motivation.* Cambridge, MA: MIT Press.

20 Bass, B. M. (Ed.). (1981). *Stogdill's handbook of leadership: A survey of theory and research* (revised and expanded version). New York, NY: The Free Press.

21 Hersey P., & Blanchard K. H. (1969). Life-cycle theory of leadership. *Training and Development Journal, 23*, 26-34. Retrieved from http://www.mendeley. com/research/life-cycle-theory-of-leadership/

22 Blanchard, Ken and Zigarmi, Drea. *Leadership and the One Minute Manager: Increasing Effectiveness Through Situational Leadership.* New York, NY: Blanchard Management Corp, 1985.

23 Burns, J. M. *Leadership.* New York, NY: Harper & Row, 1978.

24 Chrislip, David D. and Larson, Carl E. *Collaborative Leadership: How Citizens and Civic Leaders Can Make a Difference.* San Francisco, CA: Jossey-Bass, 1994.

25 Hollander, Edwin. *Inclusive Leadership: The Essential Leader-Follower Relationship.* New York, NY: Taylor & Francis, 2012.

26 George, Bill. *Discover Your True North.* New Jersey: John Wiley & Sons, Inc., 2015.

27 http://paulocoelhoblog.com/2007/12/10/the-lesson-of-the-butterfly/

28 Moore, H. G., & Galloway, J. L. (1992). *We Were Soldiers Once... and Young.* New York, NY: Random House.

29 Hesselbein, F., & Shinseki, E. K. (2004). *Be-know-do: Leadership the Army way. Adapted from the official leadership Army manual.* San Francisco, CA. Jossey Bass.

30 http://www.mohmuseum.org/site/faq

31 http://www.marriott.com/culture-and-values/j-willard-marriott.mi

32 Senge, P. (1990). *The fifth discipline: The art and practice of the learning organization.* New York, NY: Currency Doubleday.

33 Briggs, R. 0., de Vreede, G. J., and Nunamaker, J. F. Jr (2003). "Collaboration engineering with thinklets to pursue sustained success with group support systems." *Journal of Management Information Systems, 19*(4) 31-63.

34 Mitroff, I., and Featheringham, T. R. (1974). "On systemic problem solving and the error of the third kind." *Behavioral Science, 19,* 383-393

35 Townsend, Dr. John. *Leadership Beyond Reason: How Great Leaders Succeed by Harnessing the Power of Their Values, Feelings, and Intuition.* Nashville: Thomas Nelson, 2001.

36 Horsaker, David. *The Trust Edge: How Top Leaders Gain Faster Results, Deeper Relationships, and a Stronger Bottom Line.* New York: Free Press, 2012.

37 www.myemployees.com

38 http://www.we.org/